MISTAKES AND DISASTERS

Titanic Tales of Human Error and Divine Intervention

BLITZ EDITIONS

Published by Blitz Editions
an imprint of Bookmart Ltd
Registered Number 2372865
Trading as Bookmart Ltd
Desford Road
Enderby
Leicester LE9 5AD

ISBN 1 85605 102 1

This material has previously appeared in *Strange But True*
This edition reprinted 1993

Thanks to the Hulton Picture Company and
Mary Evans Picture Library for sourcing pictures.

50928/02

MISTAKES AND DISASTERS

THE TITANIC
Voyage to Disaster

They dined and danced under the glittering chandeliers ... and then they drowned in the icy North Atlantic. A single iceberg had destroyed for ever the myth of the unsinkable Titanic

She was built as the greatest ship of this or any age. Bigger, mightier, stronger, she was named *Titanic*, and she was unsinkable. The RMS *Titanic* went down on her maiden voyage in 1912, with the loss of over 1500 lives. So arrogant were the builders and operators of the gigantic vessel that they proclaimed: 'God himself could not sink this ship.' God didn't have to - all it took was a mammoth iceberg that buckled and ripped the double-steel, compartmented hull, causing the ice cold waters of the North Atlantic to flood in and sink her in just a matter of hours.

As the band played 'Nearer My God to Thee' and the ship slid below the icy, black waters, her passing seemed to mirror that of the golden age before World War I. Tom Shales, a Washington writer, said: 'The ship was not only a ship, but a time capsule, and it could be

Above: *First Officer Wilde who was on the bridge of the White Star liner when it sank beneath the waves with the loss of all but 705 of its 2227 passengers.*

Opposite: *The 46,000-ton* **Titanic** *is towed from her berth for sea trials prior to her disastrous maiden voyage in April 1912. She cost £4 million - about £100 million by today's value.*

Left: *Bruce Ismay, managing director of the White Star Line, leaves the Customs House in Southampton.*

Right: *Four towering funnels indicate the astonishing 900-ft length of the ill-fated giant of the high seas. Her height was the equivalent of an eleven-storey building.*

Below: *Some of the twenty lifeboats on the* Titanic. *Many more lives could have been saved if the liner had been equipped with more of them.*

said she took the glittery, self-indulgent golden age with her to the grave.'

But the simple, inescapable fact of the *Titanic* tragedy is that it need never have happened if the White Star Line, her owners, had equipped her with enough lifeboats. They were left off in the utter belief she could not sink.

The *Titanic* began life as the largest moving object on earth in the drawing offices of the great Harland and Wolff shipyards in Belfast, Northern Ireland; she was conceived at a time when trans-

Atlantic liner traffic was at its peak between Britain and Europe and the New World. It was to be built for luxury and speed, but not for safety.

Nevertheless, the engineers had come up with a 'revolutionary' design which would keep the ship afloat no matter what maritime accident befell it. The design was a series of watertight compartments, sixteen in all, running the length of the hull. The bulkheads separating them were also supposedly stronger and more efficient than those in use on any other ship, naval or merchant.

The makers boasted that up to two compartments could be flooded without the ship listing seriously. Not only the finest engineers, but the finest shipwrights, carpenters, tradesmen and designers were employed to make her the most luxurious vessel afloat. Everything about her was breathtaking and superlative. She was 900 feet long with four funnels, each 22 feet in diameter. From top to bottom she was the height of an eleven-storey building, and she weighed 46,000 tons. The rudder was as tall as a large mansion; the engines could produce 50,000 horsepower to move the ship at 23 knots; and there was enough electricity to power a small town.

For the first-class passengers there was unparalleled luxury. There was the first swimming pool aboard a ship - a great novelty - and a special crane which loaded and unloaded cars so the mobile millionaire could take his luxury limousine with him on a voyage. They could avail themselves of Arabian-style Turkish baths, a gym, a squash court, a lounge modelled after a room at Versailles, a Parisian cafe and a palm court.

There were sumptuous suites and cabins for 735 first-class passengers and cabins for a further 1650 passengers in second and third classes.

'The Millionaire's Special' had the first-ever swimming pool on board a ship

---

The White Star Line was proud to hype the *Titanic* as the greatest ship ever. Her passenger list for the maiden voyage from Southampton to New York read like a veritable *Who's Who* of the rich and famous of the day: there was the financier Benjamin Guggenheim, for whom the famous art museum was named in New York in a gesture to his philanthropy; Isador Straus, part owner of Macy's department store, the American painter Francis Millet and the man who built the Brooklyn Bridge.

The *Titanic* had cost £4 million to construct - equivalent today to £100 million - and she steamed under British and American flags from Southampton on her maiden voyage on 10 April 1912. On her decks were twenty lifeboats - four more than required under British Board of Trade regulations, but still woefully few for the passengers on board. Sixteen lifeboats, it was later calculated, would hold just one quarter of the passengers and crew aboard.

Survivors from the Titanic *wait to be recovered from the choppy waters of the icy North Atlantic. Few were as lucky. Those in the water died of extreme cold in two minutes.*

THE VOYAGE OF DOOM

Five days out at sea, the crew of the *Titanic* reported nothing extraordinary in the bitterly cold weather as the ship ploughed on towards the Grand Banks of Newfoundland. At night on the 14th the sea was glassy calm, but there had been sightings of icebergs in the area. They did not perturb Captain Smith, whose ship sliced through the starry night at 21.5 knots per hour.

Then, in the crow's nest, a lookout suddenly shouted at 11.40pm: 'Iceberg, right ahead!' and accompanied his shout with a warning bell that rang three times. Thirty seconds later the liner and the iceberg met in a collision that jolted the great ship, hurling ice on to the teak decks to the delight of first-class passengers who emerged moments later enthralled by the sight of the chunks of icecap littering them.

They did not know that the collision was, for the majority of them, their death knell. One of the survivors said later: 'So

Above: **American tycoon Isador Straus lost his life in the** *Titanic* **disaster. Part owner of Macy's department store, New York, he was just one of ten equally rich passengers aboard the so-called 'Millionaire's Special'.**

Above right: **Isador's wife Ida, who refused the offer of a place in a lifeboat and instead died in her husband's arms aboard the liner.**

the crash came and it sounded like this to me, like tearing a strip off a piece of calico, nothing more ... Later it grew in intensity ... as though someone had drawn a giant finger along the side of the ship.'

After the impact, first-class passengers laughed in delight at the shattered chunks of iceberg on the decks

The iceberg had risen some 90 feet out of the water and its massive submerged bulk had ripped a huge rent in the starboard section of the vessel, rupturing the watertight compartments in which so much faith had been placed. The behemoth was now taking on water at a phenomenal rate - 16,000 cubic feet of slate grey, cold Atlantic in the first forty minutes alone.

The first five compartments were completely flooded, with water slopping over into compartment 6, then compartment 7, and so on, filling them up one by one until the ship eventually sank.

On the bridge the unthinkable was slowly beginning to come home to Captain Smith, who at first could not believe his ears when his officers told him of the catastrophe taking place below. At almost exactly midnight he ordered the passengers to take to the boats while a message was flashed out that she was sinking.

Many human dramas occurred that have gone into legend; Ida Straus refused the offer of a place in a lifeboat and died in her beloved husband's arms as the liner sank beneath the waves. The chairman of the White Star Line showed no such courage and jumped into a lifeboat, thereafter forever condemned to live a life of disgrace.

Mining tycoon Guggenheim and his valet Victor Giglio dressed in evening clothes and prepared to meet their Maker like gentlemen. Ten millionaires died and valuables, including diamonds valued at £4 million, were consigned to the deep along with their owners.

Confusion reigned on the boat deck, not aided by the fact that the crewmen had never performed a proper boat drill during her sea trials. There were collapsible rafts as well as lifeboats but these were not assembled in time, or were stored in inaccessible places.

As the ship began to list dramatically distress rockets were fired into the darkness, the last faint hopes of a captain

Below: *How the news was relayed on the streets of London. The 'unsinkable' ship had met an unthinkable fate.*

Bottom: *Survivors huddle pitifully on makeshift beds. They had been picked up by the* Carpathia *which steamed belatedly to the wreck site.*

grasping for any salvation for his doomed passengers and crew. He didn't think anyone would see them - but people *did* - the crewmen aboard the passenger liner *California*, which was only nineteen miles away.

But due to incredible blunders the crew misread the distress flares as belonging to another vessel and sat in blissful ignorance in the icefield until way after five the next morning, long after the *Titanic* had slipped to her icy grave. It was later learned that the *California*'s skipper assumed that the rockets had been a false alarm.

The liner California saw the distress flares but interpreted them as a false alarm

---

The greatest tragedy on board that night befell the 670 immigrants in third class, or steerage, who were trapped below decks in doors kept locked by order of the US Immigration Department. By the time they had battered their way to the outside most of the lifeboats had slipped from their davits.

In two hours and thirty-five minutes the *Titanic* was almost at a 90-degree angle in the water, her lights twinkling and refracting on the water, casting an eerie, phosphorescent glow across the smooth sea.

Five minutes later she went under, creating a huge vortex on the surface that dragged down people and debris with it in a giant whirlpool. There was an agonizing hissing and massive air bubbles as the boilers exploded on the ship's slow descent through 13,000 feet of water.

The *Carpathia* was steaming now towards the wreck site and arrived an hour later to pick up the pitifully few survivors. Two thousand two hundred and twenty-seven people were on board the ship when it left Southampton; just 705 survived.

THE UNDERSEA GRAVE

For seventy-three years she lay undisturbed in her watery grave, a testimony to man's folly. The *Titanic*

Left: *Shock and horror soon turned to outrage and sympathy...children put money in a collecting box outside London's Mansion House.*

Opposite: *A cross-section of the* Titanic *shows how the iceberg tore through the hull between the foremast and the first funnel.*

Below: *A silent throng watches as the Lord Mayor of London arrives at St Paul's Cathedral for the memorial service to the Titanic's victims.*

became a byword for doomed ventures of heroism, cowardice, excitement and adventure. Historical societies were formed, as were survivors' associations and salvage merchants dreamed of raising her and her spoils within.

It was widely assumed that she would still be in one piece on the ocean floor when in July 1986 American oceanographer Dr Robert Ballard led an undersea team which found her. But, in the eerie, cold light, it was seen that she had broken up into three pieces - crushed by the water pressure on her descent.

In a 1600-metre debris field Ballard found the bow section, buckled under its own weight, embedded 600 metres from the stern section. In the middle was the collapsed remains of the *Titanic's* middle.

In the debris field itself are the artefacts of a lost age; an entire kitchen of copper implements, wine bottles with their corks still in them, coffee cups with the emblem of the White Star Line unfaded through the years, bathtubs, bedsprings, toilets, doorknobs, chandeliers, stoves and ceramic dolls heads that were once owned by little children who are now pensioners or long since dead.

One of the most poignant images his high-tech cameras captured was of a broken lifeboat davit, hanging limply on the edge of the ship, a silent testimony to a night that the world will never forget. A night, in fact, to remember.

FIRST CLASS STATE ROOMS

POST MAIL ROOM

THE BUCKLED PLATES

BILGE KEEL

DOUBLE BOTTOM

KEEL

ICE PENETRATING THE DOUBLE BOTTOM

KUWAIT OILFIELDS
A Dictator's Revenge

A power-hungry dictator behaving like a latter-day Hitler - but when Saddam Hussein's plans to occupy Kuwait were foiled he revenged himself on the world by unleashing environmental pollution of unimaginable magnitude

It began as a power-play, a quest for real and imagined respect among the nations of the world who would view him as a modern-day liberator. It ended in total, utter and abject defeat, with 100,000 of his countrymen dead, his nation bombed into pre-industrial bleakness, his factories reduced to ashes and twisted steel.

The Iraqi dictator Saddam Hussein's desert adventure was but a blip in history - an occupation of his neighbour Kuwait that lasted less than six months, followed by an air and ground war of less than six weeks which put paid to his grand vision as the Arab strong man seeking to find a place in the sun for all his people.

But there is no sun now on Iraq's

Above: *An Iraqi tank guards the entrance to Kuwait's Sheraton Hotel from where Europeans and Americans were rounded up.*

Opposite: *A sea of foul oil washes up on a Persian Gulf beach at the Kuwait-Saudi border. The oil had been released intentionally to hamper Desert Storm operations.*

Left: *On the first day of the invasion, 2 August 1990, Iraqi tanks stream into Kuwait City.*

Above: *Two oil-soaked cormorants on a Saudi beach near the Kuwaiti border. The birds can barely move, victims of the massive, deliberate slick measuring 8 miles by 30 miles.*

Above right: *An American marine surveys the oil-slick damage. He has turned away from a dead cormorant, suffocated by the black tide.*

horizon, or Kuwait's - it is blacked out in the stench and haze of six hundred burning oil wells.

It may be two years or more before the American and British fire-fighting teams have finally conquered each of the blown well-heads. By that time the damage to the planet may be beyond repair.

On the economic front, the Kuwaitis will have seen £100 billion worth of oil go up in smoke, and a further £25 billion worth lost in the desert sands. Nightly, on prime-time TV across the world, viewers have been given a glimpse of hell, where the fires obscure the sun at midday and young children cough their lungs out in the poisoned atmosphere. The orange fireballs roar like some mythical dragon, sending soot falling like snow across the desert wastes, blackening everything in its path.

The rain falls gooey black, mingling with the already polluted waters of the once-pristine Persian Gulf. The smoke-cloud cover makes the desert temperature 20 degrees cooler at midday and, depending on which way the wind blows, can blot out huge chunks of Kuwait City during the rush hours.

A NUCLEAR WINTER IN PROSPECT

As soon as Saddam's forces fanned out across the oilfields after his invasion of Kuwait in August 1990 the top priority for his sappers and engineers were the oil

derricks in Burgan - the second largest oilfield in the world - Wafra, Sabriya, Umm Gudair, Ahmadi, Khasman, Bahra, Rugei, Raudhaitan, Mutriba and Minagish. The Russian explosive charges on the wellheads were proof positive of his plan to make good on his threat of destruction.

Darkness at noon was just one sinister result of Saddam's deliberate devastation of the Kuwaiti oilfields

---

Some wells were exploded during the air war - the blame being put on the bombs that were poured down on Iraqi positions by allied warplanes - and the rest were set off at twenty second intervals as the coalition's armoured spearheads smashed through the defences at breakneck speed.

The liberation of Kuwait thus took place under a black sky, in an atmosphere dangerous to breathe.

The well fires are sustained by the huge natural pressure from beneath the desert surface in the oil reservoir, pushing the oil to the surface at speeds of one thousand miles per hour.

Five hundred thousand tons of oil-related pollutants are spewed out daily by the oil well fires - ten times the amount emitted by all American industrial and power-generating plants combined. Toxic chemicals, including hydrogen sulphide, sulphur dioxide, carbon monoxide and hydrocarbons, are among the deadly particles trapped in the black, oily smoke.

HUMAN AND ECOLOGICAL VICTIMS

The smoke may yet trigger one of the deadliest scenarios in the environmental lexicon - a nuclear winter where the smoke rises into the atmosphere to cut off sunlight and air, turning parts of the earth into permafrost zones.

Above: *As allied forces continued to advance on Kuwait City in February 1991, Iraqi prisoners were led away from the desert in their thousands.*

Below: *Smoke and flames from burning Kuwaiti oil wells were visible for scores of miles around.*

At ground level, the burning oil wells threaten the delicate ecosystem of the desert itself. Although a desert may seem a lifeless place, it is in fact home to myriad species of insects, scorpions and snakes as well as to larger animals such as camels and gazelles. Micro-organisms form a crust on the desert floor in much the same way as coral forms under the sea. This crust catches the seeds of shrubs and prevents the sand from blowing away.

Now over 300 square miles of desert lies under oil - some of it inches deep, others vast lakes six feet and more in depth - the result of spewing gushers that did not ignite when the retreating Iraqis blew the wellheads.

It will be decades before the full ecological effects of these oil lakes can be evaluated, but in the short term they spell catastrophe for the desert's fragile infrastructure. Where the surface has not been flooded by oil it has been turned into sheets of glass, the result of searing 4000 degree temperatures.

The first victims of the smoke are people with respiratory problems. Asthma and bronchitis sufferers are already queuing up for aid in Kuwait and as far away as Bahrain, where the smog drifts when the wind blows in the wrong direction.

But far more worrying are the fears

about future generations. Because of the high volume of cancer-causing agents trapped in the smoke, doctors say babies could be born deformed, in much the same way that the escape of radiation at the Chernobyl power plant in the Soviet Union has triggered an appalling number of mutations in both human beings and animals.

FIGHTING THE FIRES

But that is a problem for the future. Currently firefighters from Texas, Britain and Belgium are battling the blazes at what seems at times like an agonizingly slow pace. Wearing nothing more hi-tech than cotton overalls, the £600 per day firefighters are slowly dousing the wells, using a combination of guts, brute force and wily know-how gleaned from tackling oil fires around the globe.

Under a constant barrage of water, they move towards the intense heat of the flames in cranes shielded with tin sheeting. Using either dynamite to blow out the flames or specially moulded steel to snuff them out, they then move in with a new set of valves called a Christmas Tree which they fit on to the pipe and gradually close to form a seal. One mistake and they will be blown sky-high.

Above: *Workmen dug fresh graves in Kuwait City's Raqqua cemetery as victims caught up in the fighting were discovered.*

Right: *The picture that told the world that the Gulf War was over. Thousands of Iraqi vehicles - private and military - had been blasted by allied forces.*

Red Adair, the Texan oil firefighter who bravely led his men against the inferno on the Piper Alpha oil rig disaster in the North Sea which claimed over a hundred lives, is awed by the spectacle of the burning wellheads. He said:

Each one in its own right would be a disaster. And we have hundreds of them to deal with. We have to improvise every step of the way - there is nothing cast in stone about how each one must be tackled. People who say we are not working fast enough don't know the power that we are dealing with. The job is as tough as hell and we are working seven days a week.

Even so, it could be two years before the fires are extinguished and the wellheads capped.

MARINE POLLUTION

No less of an environmental disaster has been created by Saddam and his forces in the Persian Gulf - again the target of the Iraqi dictator's unique brand of eco-terrorism. More than 460 million gallons of unrefined crude oil were leaked into the waters that are home to thousands of fish and seabirds and were once rich fishing grounds harvested by Arabs from several nations. Shrimp beds have been decimated, and the breeding grounds of rare marine life lost forever. The damage is truly incalculable.

The slick is still there, months after the end of the war. Thousands of seabirds and fish have died, the TV images of their bloated, pathetic bodies bobbing on oil-thick waves evoking more sympathy in Western nations than did the Iraqi dead on the road to Basra at the war's end.

Millions of gallons of oil have been skimmed from the Gulf already, but millions more have washed ashore to bake in the hot climate, forming a permanent tar pavement over beaches.

An estimated twenty thousand or more seabirds have died so far. The spring months are the worst, as forty-five different species of birds use the Gulf as a refuelling spot on the northward migration from Africa and Arabia to their summer breeding grounds in northern Europe, the sub-Arctic and beyond. Many of these sandpipers, plovers, redshanks and others will die in the fouled waters for years to come. One or two, like the red-necked phalarope, might even be lost altogether to their native breeding grounds.

A BLEAK FUTURE?

Dr Hassan Nasrallah, a climatologist, warns that the final consequences of the environmental disaster in Kuwait may not be understood for decades. He said:

We are talking about massive sources of pollution of a kind that have never been monitored before. The world has no experience of a conflagration of the kind which has engulfed Kuwait. Humankind has done this awful thing to the planet and humankind will have to see what permanent damage has been done.

Below: *Long after the fighting was over, the oil fields of Kuwait continued to burn, lighting up the skies and polluting the entire region.*

THE HINDENBURG
Flames in the Sky

The airship Hindenburg was built in the thirties as a symbol of Hitler's new Germany, and her safety procedures were second to none. So why did she explode in a blazing inferno in May 1937?

The *Hindenburg* was by far the most luxurious airship of all time, a floating palace dedicated to comfort, grandeur and efficiency as she ferried her wealthy clientele across the Atlantic.

She was so vast and so graceful, that she was to aviation what the once-mighty *Titanic* had been to shipping. And ironically, like the great liner which had sunk below the icy waters of the Atlantic Ocean twenty-five years earlier, the *Hindenburg*, too, was destined for disaster.

As she approached her dock at the Lakehurst naval station in New Jersey in May 1937, the great airship exploded into a fiery ball. Flames swept through the 198,000 cubic metres of highly inflammable hydrogen which filled the belly of the craft. In a scant thirty-two seconds the *Hindenburg*, more than twice the length of a football field, had been reduced to a charred skeleton of twisted metal. And in her death throes she had taken thirty-six people with her.

What happened? Was it an act of God, or was it sabotage? Even today, over half a century later, the answer remains as much a riddle as it did then.

HITLER'S FLAGSHIP

The tragic events of 6 May 1937 came just two years after the *Hindenburg* was completed, and less than twelve months after her first test flight. Symbolizing the

Above: *The promenade deck of the* Hindenburg, *literally the last word in air travel luxury in the 1930s.*

Opposite: *The huge bulk of the new airship fills its hangar. Her proud builders regarded her as the safest means of flight in the world.*

Below: *She was to the skies what the* Titanic *had been to the high seas. Both behemoths, however, were equally ill-fated.*

Above: *Proudly marked with the Nazis' swastika emblem, the tail of Hitler's flagship, the* Hindenburg *protrudes from its hangar.*

rise of the Third Reich, she was considered a national treasure, the largest, most expensive dirigible ever made. To the Fuehrer, Adolf Hitler, she was incontrovertible proof of the Aryan supremacy he so often bragged about.

To her builders, however, she was more than a showpiece of Nazi Germany. She was also the safest means of flight, fitted out with the most advanced security measures then available.

Regulations obliged both crew and passengers to hand over their matches and lighters before boarding

---

Indeed, safety measures were even more stringent than on other vessels. The crew wore anti-static overalls and shoes soled with hemp, and all those aboard - including passengers - had to hand over

their matches and lighters before they were allowed to board.

The airship's safety mechanisms were matched only by the grandeur of her many facilities, including quiet, comfortable state rooms.

The bar served the speciality of the ship, the LZ-129 Frosted Cocktail - gin with a dash of orange juice that took its name from the formal designation of the *Hindenburg*.

The meals were prepared by the finest chefs that Germany had to offer, and served on blue and gold porcelain. There was even a specially constructed, lightweight piano aboard for entertainment.

Most of the pampered passengers, however, preferred to spend their time relaxing in the observation room or cupola - a room enclosed by windows and attached to the craft's underbelly.

have been taken hold by a number of men in the field. The back motors of the ship are holding it just enough to keep it... it's burst into flame! This is terrible! The flames are 500 feet into the sky...

Then, choking back tears, he forced himself to continue: 'This is the worst thing I've ever witnessed. It is one of the worst catastrophes in the world. Oh, the humanity! All the passengers! I don't believe it!'

'It's a terrible crash,' he concluded. 'It's just lying there, a massive smoking

'A MASSIVE SMOKING WRECK'

Everything seemed to be going smoothly on 6 May 1937, as the giant craft passed so low over the Manhattan skyline that passengers waving from open windows in her vast silver belly came almost face to face with news photographers perched atop the Empire State Building.

But as the *Hindenburg* neared the Lakehurst naval station several hours late, after being buffeted by high winds on her eleventh transatlantic crossing, tragedy struck. Just seconds after her guide-ropes had been lowered for mooring and eventual landing, she exploded into a towering inferno above the stunned crowd which had gathered to greet the giant airship. The explosion was so loud that it could be heard fifteen miles away.

As the hydrogen in the Hindenburg's belly ignited, the explosion was heard fifteen miles away

---

Well-known radio reporter Herbert Morrison, on hand to describe the *Hindenburg*'s arrival in a broadcast to the American people, gave what is still considered to be the definitive description of the disaster.

As the huge airship neared, he began his report:

The ropes have been dropped and they

Above: *The* **Hindenburg** *was the largest - and most expensive - dirigible ever made.*

Right: *Forget sea travel ... this was the new way to span the globe in the optimistic Thirties.*

Below right: *The Hindenburg was a 'hotel' in the sky, with every comfort of a luxury liner.*

wreck.' Before their eyes, and those of other horrified witnesses, the *Hindenburg* was quickly consumed by the inferno, which fed itself on the vast hydrogen bags kept in its belly. Panicked passengers and crew jumped from the windows and doors to the ground below in a mad dash to escape the flames as the airship lurched and thrashed. The smell of burning flesh and the screams of the dying filled the night air. Meanwhile, as pandemonium was erupting all about him, Commander Max Pruss, a seasoned Zeppelin pilot, did his best to right the ship. He did not abandon the vessel until it crashed to the ground. Miraculously, Pruss and sixty-one other passengers and crew survived the disaster.

WHAT WENT WRONG?

What had turned the safest means of transportation yet known into a death trap? As reporters and concerned citizens scrambled for an answer, an official board of inquiry was set up to probe the disaster and try to pinpoint the cause of the fire.

At first the commission focused on the possibility of sabotage - not unlikely given the *Hindenburg*'s status as a showpiece of the hated Third Reich. Once sabotage had been ruled out, the commission considered numerous other possible causes, including leaking gas valves, static electricity and engine sparks. But nothing proved definitive.

Despite the outcry, however, the file on the *Hindenburg* disaster was closed. It would remain so until eight years later, after the end of World War II, when it finally emerged that the Nazis had wielded a strong influence over the official inquiry.

In fact, it become known that Hermann Goering, head of the Luftwaffe and once heir apparent to Hitler, had actually ordered the commission not to investigate the possibility of sabotage too thoroughly. The destruction of a Nazi symbol was embarrassment enough. Aryan pride could not take another blow by admitting that a saboteur had been responsible.

That possibility was raised again some thirty-five years later, when Michael

Right: *As it approached its mooring at Lakehurst naval station, an explosion of flames began to engulf the Hindenburg.*

Below: *'This is terrible,' announced radio commentator Herbert Morrison. 'The flames are 500 feet into the sky.'*

MacDonald Mooney claimed in his book that the disaster was no accident, but planned destruction by a young anti-Nazi saboteur. He identified the perpetrator as Erich Spehl, a twenty-five-year-old blond, blue-eyed airship rigger from the Black Forest, who perished in the flames.

He also alleged that both German and American officials agreed to the cover-up because they did not want to spark 'an international incident'. Although it can never be proved for certain that the *Hindenburg* was sabotaged and that Spehl was the misguided culprit, one thing can be stated beyond a doubt. The tragedy was the finale of an era when luxury was prized as greatly as speed.

Immediately after the crash, Germany halted all commercial Zeppelin services.

The *Hindenburg*'s sister ship, the LZ-130 or *Graf Zeppelin II*, was none the less completed - but Hitler's new-found antagonism towards airships soon led to the scrapping of all Zeppelins and ended the airship programme.

Eventually the *Graf Zeppelin II* was used to carry out spying missions against Britain. Interestingly, the *Hindenburg*, too, became part of the German war effort. The wreckage of the once-proud airship, which had peacefully plied the skies in quiet serenity, was shipped back to Germany - and recycled into war planes.

Below: *The* **Hindenburg'***s burnt-out remains. Miraculously 62 passengers and crew survived; 36 people perished.*

SEVESO
Cloud of Death

In July 1976 the little Italian town of Seveso was the victim of a terrible accident at the local chemical plant. A deadly cloud of poison gas was discharged into the atmosphere, and its effects may last for generations

Right: *Frightened, bewildered, the people of Seveso were evacuated after their town was contaminated in July 1976.*

Opposite: *Masked specialists worked day and night in an almost futile attempt to clean up the chemical plant.*

For years after 'it' happened, the ghost town of Seveso in Northern Italy still idled like some gigantic science-fiction movie set, shuttered behind a Berlin Wall of environmental quarantine panels. 'CONTAMINATED AREA - NO ADMITTANCE' read notices in five languages. Across the top of the panels

Below: *Animals and plants over many square miles were affected when a safety valve burst at the Seveso chemical factory...which then billowed out its poisonous cloud.*

and into the scarred area hung limp telephone cables attached to the sides of the humble houses within.

But the phones did not ring any more, for there was no one to answer them. The core of Seveso was a dead zone, snuffed out in one of mankind's worst chemical accidents. It would become known as the Italian Hiroshima.

It happened on 10 July 1976, when an explosion at the Swiss-owned Icmesa

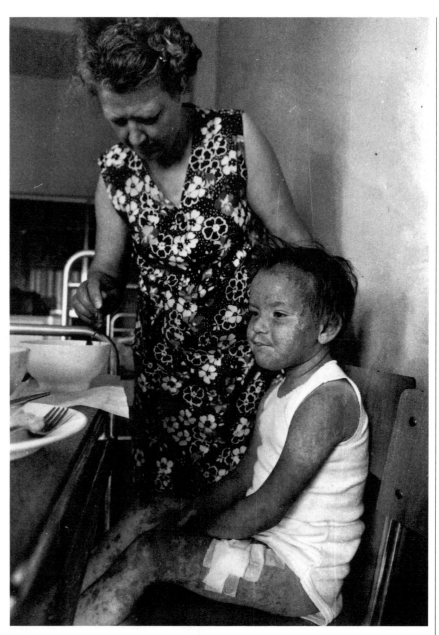

Above: *Little Alice Senno, aged four, was one of the many young victims of the poison gas cloud that escaped from the chemical plant near her home.*

chemical plant discharged a thick white cloud of dioxin, one of the deadliest poisons known to man, over about six square miles of the small industrial suburb some thirteen miles from Milan. As the poison settled on homes and gardens in the following days thousands of pets died, crops were infected and hundreds of people developed nausea, blurred vision and a disfiguring disease known as chloracne.

As at Chernobyl, which came after it, human error unleashed on the unsuspecting innocents of Seveso a man-made disaster of epic proportions.

Dioxin is a by-product of trichlorophenol, used in germicides, deodorants and soaps. Four ounces in the water

supply of a major city would be enough to wipe out 8 million people; on that black summer day there was enough released in its concentrated form to wipe out 100 million. The long term effects upon the blighted land and the unborn babies of future generations have still to be assessed.

A STRANGE WHISTLING NOISE

The seventeen thousand residents of Seveso, a town nestling in the green foothills of the Po valley, still had plenty of countryside around them to offset the sprawling factories which fanned out from Milan.

At the plant, which employed many local people, Viro Romani, a technician, was just finishing his lunch. Since it was a Saturday there was no active production going on at the works, so only ten of the 160 employees were on duty.

The firm, a subsidiary of the massive Hoffman-La Roche pharmaceutical companies - one of the world's largest - used the trichlorophenol, or TCP, for the manufacture of hexachlorophene, the active ingredient in many soaps. Hexachlorophene had been banned in the USA but was still widely used in a number of other nations.

The plant's chemical reactor was closed that day, but as Viro Romani sipped his coffee in the canteen there was a loud bang followed by an eerie, piercing whistling. The men ran outside in time to witness the escape of the lethal dioxin, which spewed out at tremendous pressure from the safety valves on top of the apparatus.

Families preparing lunch were suddenly seized by fits of coughing as the cloud rolled over them

---

Within minutes fine particles of the chemical were falling like snow while the air filled with the pungent smell of chlorine. As emergency taps were turned on to pour cold water inside the reactor the cloud rolled away gently over the Italian countryside on its ominous journey. Families sitting at cafes in the streets or making lunch in their homes

Left: *Notices were hastily erected to 'quarantine' the area around Seveso. They remained in place for years afterwards.*

Below: *Italian soldiers erect barbed wire fencing around the polluted area of Seveso. Meanwhile hundreds of people were bundled on to evacuation buses.*

were suddenly stricken with fits of coughing and tears rolled down their cheeks. Later in the day, when the cloud had moved on, they complained of headaches and nausea, and a lingering, acrid smell like burned plastic hanging in the air.

WHY DID IT HAPPEN?

During the first twenty-four hours after the explosion the officials of the plant began their inquest into what had gone wrong. It seemed that the heat of the chemical reaction from the previous day's production had not cooled properly.

To deal with this potential problem, most companies have safety valves like the ones installed at the Seveso plant, and back them up with enormous dump tanks ready to absorb lethal poisons before they can be discharged into the atmosphere. But Seveso had no such dump tanks, and the safety valve not only failed at the crucial moment, but was located on the vent pipe leading to the roof. The result was the escape of the gas.

IMMEDIATE EFFECTS

It was only after the first three or four days that the full impact of what had happened began to hit home. By Wednesday the doctors' surgeries in Seveso were crammed with people - many of them children - suffering an abundance of ugly rashes and weeping boils, complaining of backache, sickness and blinding headaches.

Patients told the doctors that animals and birds in their gardens and vegetable plots had been dying suddenly. An old man saw three robins on his grass just keel over and die, as if the will to live had gone. Cats and dogs would walk down the street and drop dead. Tomato plants and maize fields seemed burned, the vegetation dry and crumbling, while in the pastures the stricken cattle began bleeding from their eyes and ears. Entire chicken roosts were destroyed, the pathetic carcasses rotting in the summer heat.

Doctors began to grow angry at the lack of information from factory bosses. News about it travelled slowly. There had been no huge explosion, no fire, to warrant the accident reaching the prime-time news broadcasts, so the company stayed silent.

It was on Friday, when a two-year-old baby was rushed into the local hospital, a mass of blisters and rashes, that the mayors of Seveso and nearby Meda pressed Icmesa officials for some answers. The company bosses worriedly said that the soil samples were being examined by boffins in Switzerland, but admitted that posters and warning notices about not eating local produce should be posted around town.

Overnight another eighteen children were taken to hospital and by now a state approaching panic was beginning to grip the innocent citizens of Seveso.

Birds were now no longer dropping in ones or twos from the sky, but in whole flocks. The animals seemed to be suffering more quickly than the humans, probably because they ate grass, drank rainwater and were generally closer to the fall-out of dioxin than were people. But the doctors, relying on information supplied by the company, were treating the patients as if they had been exposed to TCP - a mild irritant and a million times less toxic than dioxin.

THE TRUTH DISCOVERED

Bruno Ambrosi, a newsman working in Milan, had a university knowledge of chemistry and found out that dioxin was manufactured in TCP when the temperature of the chemical goes over 200 degrees.

That, he discovered chillingly, is exactly what had happened.

One paper he read about it said: 'It is the most potent small-molecule toxin known to man. Its effects dwarf those of arsenic and strychnine.' Dioxin attacked the liver and kidneys and it was also 'mutagenic' - it had the power to change the chromosomes in the body, leading to cancer and to birth defects in unborn children.

Ambrosi broke the story just as the Swiss scientists confirmed what he already knew to be true - that massive amounts of dioxin had escaped and leached into the soil and atmosphere, with catastrophic effects. Dioxin was insoluble in water, and once it penetrated a substance it could stay there for years.

STATE OF EMERGENCY

An emergency centre was set up in an elementary school, and local health workers were drafted in to run it. Eight days after the accident the Italian government declared a state of emergency.

Vittoria Rivolta, health minister in the province of Lombardy, began correlating the data on a huge map to try to chart where the cloud had gone and so

Below: *An Italian carabiniere feeds a cow. But like thousands of other farm creatures contaminated by the escaping poison, it had to be destroyed later.*

years thousands of tons of soil were removed and buried in concrete, while thousands of tons of plants and seventy thousand animal corpses were burned. Refugees were relocated in temporary accommodation, compensated for loss of produce and property, and promised new housing equal to that which they had abandoned.

Most of the 736 families evacuated were eventually returned to their homes, but 256 people were permanently locked out of the exclusion area in Zone A, where dioxin levels were the highest. An official report three years later by the Italian parliament damned the operators of the chemical plant. It said the plant was unsafe to begin with, and revealed that company officials waited twenty-seven hours after the accident before notifying even the most minor municipal official. The company went on to pay some £8 million pounds in compensation.

Miraculously, no humans have yet died. Some babies have been born with mutated insides, but it is not yet clear whether they have been the victims of dioxin. All but two of the 187 children stricken with chloracne recovered.

determine how far the dioxin had spread. On Saturday, 24 July there was a total evacuation from Zone A in the town, an area on Rivolta's map that suffered the most sickness among humans and the most deaths among animals. Two hundred families left the area, which was then cordoned off by police and caribinieri with six miles of barbed wire. Then the men, wearing protective suits, moved through the area killing every creature still left alive in it. At the end of the killing over fifty thousand animals had been slaughtered. There were a further ten thousand corpses from the effects of the dioxin poisoning.

Above: *The disastrous effects of the poison cloud can clearly be seen on these leaves. The chemical had previously been used as a defoliant in Vietnam.*

FEARS FOR THE FUTURE

Dr Anne Walker, a dermatologist who had treated workers in previous dioxin accidents, said the full effects of the tragedy might not show up for two decades. Fear and uncertainty spread among the population.

As thousands upon thousands of tests were carried out on the local people, and they were graded into high-risk, middle-risk and low-risk categories, the Italian government authorized abortions in the region for fear of abnormal births adding to the disaster. Over a period of two

Right: *Animals were generally affected more quickly than humans. Dogs and cats were collected in dustbin liners, as were birds which had fallen from the sky.*

CHERNOBYL
Nuclear Nightmare

Massive radiation readings in Sweden. Then days of Soviet silence about what had really happened. This was the worst disaster the nuclear power industry has ever known - Chernobyl

The first indication that something had gone wrong - terribly, irredeemably wrong - occurred at 9am on Monday, 28 April 1986, as boffins at the Forsmark nuclear power station, sixty miles from the Swedish capital of Stockholm, noticed disturbing signals bleeping on their ghost-green screens.

The signals were measures of radiation, and the horrified scientists feared a massive reactor leak at the power plant entrusted to their high-tech care. A careful and methodical check of all equipment and its monitoring gauges showed no leakage - and yet the sensors indicated that the air they were breathing was four times the ordained safe limit.

Geiger counters were hurriedly deployed for swift checks on all six hundred workers. The readings were haywire, showing that virtually every worker had been exposed to radiation way above safe limits.

Outside it was the same story - samples taken from soil and plant life showed extraordinarily high deposits of radioactive material. Sweden and much of Europe was being infected by a silent, unseen, unscented killer.

Sixty-seven-and-a-half hours earlier Lieutenant-Colonel Leonid Telyatnikov had been enjoying a few well-earned days off when the telephone rang at his home seventy-five miles outside Kiev in the Soviet Ukraine at 1.32am on 26 April. A breathless voice informed him that there had been an 'incident' at the Chernobyl nuclear power plant eighty miles from Kiev.

It was a bright, starlit night as Telyatnikov, leading his crew of twenty-eight firefighters, raced to the scene. A bright orange glow soon appeared on the horizon. 'I had no idea what had happened or what we were heading into,' recalled Telyatnikov. 'But as I approached the plant I could see debris on fire all around like sparklers.

'Then I noticed a bluish glow above the wreckage of reactor four and pockets of fire on surrounding buildings. It was absolutely silent and eerie.' Protected by no more than wellington boots and a hard hat, Telyatnikov, later honoured as a Hero of the Soviet Union, was confronting the worst disaster in thirty-two years of commercial nuclear power's history.

A WHOLE CONTINENT OF VICTIMS

The partial meltdown of the Chernobyl nuclear reactor caused a tragedy that continues to bring death, suffering and misery to this day. Untold thousands have died from tumours and cancer caused by the explosion. Human beings, cattle and other livestock, have given birth to nightmarish offspring, deformed and mutated by the effects of the radiation. The earth has been scarred forever, and

Opposite: *In the early hours of 26 April 1986, it became apparent that a dreadful disaster had occurred at the Chernobyl nuclear power plant near Kiev.*

Below: *By the time scientists had arrived to examine the damage, a cloud of nuclear poison was already drifting westwards towards Sweden.*

mankind left to ponder whether the benefits of nuclear energy are not outweighed by the spectre of such a disaster ever occurring again.

By the time the Forsmark scientists had discovered the presence of massive amounts of radiation in the atmosphere, strong winds were carrying it all over Europe. Light rain fell on the salt marshes of Brittany, making the milk in cows' udders toxic. Heavier rain poured down on to the Welsh hillsides, making the tender lamb forbidden flesh. Snow in Finland, Sweden and West Germany was infected too.

The Swedish scientists informed their government that they believed the source for this nuclear volcano, spewing its lethal residue into the skies, was the Soviet Union. But Communist Russia remained silent.

It was not until 9pm Moscow time that night when the Kremlin finally admitted that something had happened - but it gave no indication of the gravity of the mishap. A terse four-sentence statement was read on the evening news in Moscow.

Almost grudging in its admission, the statement said: 'An accident has taken place at the Chernobyl power station and one of the reactors was damaged. Measures are being taken to eliminate the consequences of the accident. Those affected by it are being given assistance. A government commission has been set up.' The announcer then picked up another sheet of paper and went on to read a story about a Soviet peace fund.

Moscow's first official announcement was a cover-up - a four-line statement on the nightly news

---

Western governments began to exert diplomatic pressure on the Soviet Union for details of exactly what had happened. But only men like Telyatnikov knew in those first few hours the enormity of the disaster. 'I realized it was not an ordinary situation as soon as I passed through the gate,' he said. 'There was just the noise of machines and the fire crackling. The firefighters knew what they had to do and proceeded quietly, on the run. The

Above: *Workers go about their duties in a reactor room of the Chernobyl plant. This picture was taken in 1982, four years before the disaster.*

radiation-measuring meters had frozen on their highest level. Thoughts of my family would flash through my mind and be gone. No one would discuss the radiation risk. The most frightening thought was that we wouldn't have enough strength to hold out until reserves came. About an hour after the fire began a group of fire-fighters with symptoms of radiation exposure were taken down from a rooftop close to the damaged reactor. When I approached five men to take up the position they rushed to the rooftop almost before I could get the words out of my mouth. They are all dead now, from radioactive poisoning.'

Telyatnikov too is one of what the

Ukrainians call 'the living dead'. He began vomiting even as he fought the flames and since then has battled cancer, like thousands of others.

The burning white-hot graphite core of the reactor blazed at 5000 degrees Fahrenheit - twice the temperature of molten steel - and thrust millions of cubic feet of radioactive gas into the atmosphere. Pictures taken by a CIA satellite four hundred miles above the earth were on President Ronald Reagan's desk forty-eight hours after the red alert was sounded by the Forsmark scientists. They showed a picture of hell that the embarrassed, technologically inept Soviets, refused to admit publicly.

In the immediate hours after the tragedy Per Olof Sjostedt, technical and scientific adviser at the Swedish embassy in Moscow, contacted officials of the Soviet nuclear energy programme armed with the information given to him via the Forsmark scientists. He was curtly told that there was no information to be had.

It took rising Soviet politician Boris Yeltsin to step forward several days later to lend gravity to his government's so far casual response to the disaster. He said: 'It is serious. Very serious. The cause apparently lies in human error. We are undertaking measures to make sure this doesn't happen again.'

The whole area within an eighteen-mile radius of Chernobyl was evacuated and declared an unfit zone, where cattle, drinking water and vegetation were all deemed unfit for consumption.

MELTDOWN

Nuclear physicists began to theorize about what had happened at the Chernobyl reactor and came up with a likely scenario. The reactor used uranium fuel rods to generate heat used to boil water into steam. The steam in turn powered turbine generators for power. Cooling water is essential in such a system to stop the fuel rods from super-heating, causing a meltdown or burn-up, in which the core virtually turns itself into a nuclear bomb.

It seems that the water circulation system to provide the cooling liquid had failed, causing the temperature in the reactor core to hit 5000 degrees. The uranium fuel rods melted and produced radioactive steam that reacted with the zirconium alloy cladding of the rods to produce explosive hydrogen gas.

Soviet officials proved reluctant to seek outside assistance while still trying to pretend that not much had happened. But a Soviet scientific officer attached to their embassy in Bonn did approach the West German nuclear power industry with a request for information on fighting graphite core fires. A similar request went out the same day to Swedish authorities, and Moscow invited Californian bone marrow expert Dr Robert Gale to provide medical aid to Chernobyl victims.

'Please tell the world to help us!' cried an anguished Russian voice picked up by a Dutch radio ham

---

Moscow tackled the blaze with an army of workers and soldiers - most of them now dead or suffering from the effects of prolonged exposure to such massive dosages of radiation. Helicopters carrying tons of wet sand and

Below: *Three months after the blast, clean-up crews hang chunks of graphite from a burnt-out nuclear reactor. Their 'protective' clothing failed to save many of them from cancer and death.*

lead flew over the site and dumped their loads directly on to the blazing reactor. Tons of the element boron, which absorbs neutrons, was also dumped on to the smouldering fires.

THE TERRIBLE AFTERMATH

By the end of the week the fire was out - but so was the radiation, incalculable amounts of it, spreading an ominous pall over Europe and the western half of the Soviet Union. On the ground, near to the site, the victims began dying of haemorrhages and brain seizures. They were often the lucky ones - the lingering deaths, the mutated stillborn babies, the cancer which racks heroes like fireman Telyatnikov, were yet to come.

In a bid to clean up some of the debris the Soviets dug a huge pit and filled it with shattered remnants of the reactor, twisted metal and broken concrete from the plant and clothes worn by disaster workers. Some 2 million cubic feet of concrete was mixed over the next six weeks and poured on to the reactor, sealing it forever.

As the rescuers struggled, President Reagan became angrier with Moscow, and said so in a nationwide radio address. He told America in his usual Saturday speech: 'The Soviets owe the world an explanation. A full accounting of what happened at Chernobyl and what is happening now is the least the world community has a right to expect.'

Nuclear experts declared the RBMK-1000 reactors at Chernobyl mighty but outdated machines. But most glaringly, said the experts, the Russians showed a distinct lack of care about safety by not building the reactor with a concrete outer structure that could have contained most of the fire and the subsequent radiation.

Ten times as much radiation escaped as at Hiroshima and Nagasaki

---

It is now known that over a hundred thousand people were evacuated from the region. Even the government newspaper *Izvestia* has admitted that as many as 3 million people are still living on irradiated land, selling as well as devouring their produce. After four years of bureaucratic book-cooking, health statistics show an increase in blood disorders, freak offspring and deformed plant life that is unlike anything else found on earth.

Dr Gale, who provided much of the medical expertise the Russians needed for bone marrow transplants on victims, predicts as many as 150,000 new cancer cases in the next ten years as a direct result of the Chernobyl fall-out. In Minsk alone the incidences of leukaemia have doubled in five years.

Due to the outdated technology and stagnant economy of the country, just a fraction of this number will be cured.

FEAR AND MISTRUST

Chernobyl's most lasting legacy will be the mistrust felt by the country's own citizens about a workers' paradise that condemned people to die with dis-information and disorganization.

Crude technology and disregard for safety were held to blame

As to blame for the tragedy, the Soviets were quick to find scapegoats. The former director of the plant, Viktor Bryukhanov, and the former chief engineer, Anatoly Dyatlov, in charge of doomed reactor number four, were both asleep when the cooling system failed and the reactor blew up at 1.23am. They were consequently jailed for dereliction of duty. Two others received three-year prison terms, and two more suspended sentences.

SICK IRONY

As a macabre postscript to the tragedy of Chernobyl, the Kiev authorities are offering to take death-wish tourists on a tour of the devastated nuclear power plant. Ever hungry for hard currency, the local tourist bureau apparatchiks are hoping to lure Westerners to the dead zone with advertising that promises fairground-type thrills:

*CHILL to the eerie dead city of Chernobyl as you walk through deserted

schools, farms and factories!

*GASP in awe at the tomb of the great melted reactor, now encased in tons of concrete!

*SWOON at the sight of the mutated farm animals born with horrifying defects as a result of the fall-out!

And as if to prove their social responsibility, the organizers behind this macabre voyeurism promise takers of the tour a full medical examination afterwards to check for radiation poisoning. Part of the tour - that will cost up to £200 for a single day - includes visits to the farms and homes where comrades have defied the Kremlin and returned to the land after the explosion.

It is highly unlikely that the land and buildings are completely free from radioactivity.

Some scientists believe that it could be up to a hundred years before the radiation levels have dropped sufficiently for it not to pose a potential health threat. Thirty-seven died in the reactor explosion and

fire. But thousands more have died from radiation poisoning and cancers triggered by the fall-out. Scientist Dr David Abrahamovitz said: 'If tourists were to go there, say, after a rainfall, there would be more chance of a higher radiation level registering than if they went when it was dry because the water would release more toxins in the dry earth. It is not a visit that I would be queuing up to go on.'

Excursion officials say they will also take in the little town of Slavutich, a radiation workers' colony that is home to the people who monitor the dead zone and ensure that the radioactive pile is not leaking from its concrete tomb. The motto of the town is: 'Life is good - but too short!'

American writer Francis Clines said: 'The notion has the virtue of dark candour, of daring to think the outside world might like to at least leer, if not memorialize, an historic outrage upon one of the earth's humbler landscapes.'

Above: *It took years for the full horror of the Chernobyl disaster to be revealed. 'The problems will unfold well into the next century,' says Soviet scientist Igor Ignatchev.*

ZEEBRUGGE FERRY
Tragedy in the Channel

A short ferry crossing on a familiar stretch of water became a night of hell for crew and passengers. In March 1987 the Herald of Free Enterprise sank as she left port

Right: *As dawn broke over the Belgian port of Zeebrugge, the full scale of the tragedy of 6 March 1987 became apparent.*

Opposite: *The* **Herald of Free Enterprise** *set sail from Zeebrugge with her bow doors open. It was a recipe for an unparalleled tragedy in maritime history.*

The English Channel is the world's busiest waterway. Each day the narrow sea lane separating Britain from continental Europe is negotiated by thousands of vessels of all shapes, sizes and nationalities. For holidaymakers the ferries which ply between the British, French, Belgian and Dutch ports are regarded as little more than lumbering omnibuses, making the journey with such regularity and such apparent ease that it is often forgotten that the Channel is the graveyard of countless ships, lost in waters that are dangerous and cold.

Weather has undoubtedly played a great part in claiming the lives of stricken vessels. But so too has human error. And it was an appalling chain of human errors - what an official inquiry would later brand forever as 'the disease of sloppiness' - which struck the *Herald of*

Below: *Passengers had no time to don lifejackets as the ferry rolled on its side, hurling them into the freezing waters in pitch darkness.*

Free Enterprise as she steamed for Dover from the Belgian port of Zeebrugge on 6 March 1987.

Due to that 'disease of sloppiness', the bow doors of the Townsend Thoresen car ferry were left open as she steamed into the night. Water poured in, unstoppably, flooding the car decks before tilting the ship to a list that was irreversible. She rolled on to her side, saved from sinking only by a shallow sandbank, and in the confusion and chaos that followed 193 people lost their lives.

The agony of that night has been played over and over again in the minds of those who survived, those who were the rescuers, those who saw it on TV, and those who were left to judge the men who caused it.

'IT'S DEFINITELY GOING OVER'

The *Herald of Free Enterprise* was a 7951-ton ferry, 132 metres long and part of the Blue Riband fleet operated by Townsend which crossed the Channel in record times. Time, it was later to be learned, was a critical operating factor with Townsend bosses. On the highly competitive Channel routes, turnaround and speed at sea were of the essence if Townsend was to stay ahead of rival shipping lines.

When she steamed out of Zeebrugge that night Captain David Lewry was at the helm. An experienced skipper and a long-time employee of Townsend Thoresen, Captain Lewry was on the

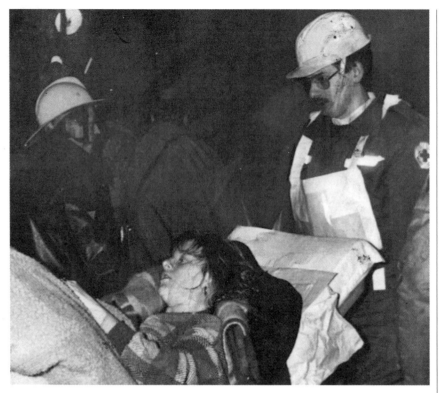

Above: *The ferry lurched like a giant whale, throwing passengers across decks, shops, lounges, bars and restaurants. The injured were carried out shocked and disorientated.*

looked back at it, it looked like something out of the Second World War that was hit with torpedoes.'

A lorry driver looked back and thought the stricken ship looked as if she had been hit by torpedoes

Many of the people on board were day trippers taking advantage of an offer from Britain's biggest popular newspaper, the *Sun,* to sail cheaply, on a day return ticket costing £1. One of them, Andrew Simmons, 30, of Bushey, near Watford, recalled: 'We were trapped for twenty or thirty minutes after the boat went over. Within a minute it went from being upright to on its side with water gushing in down the stairs and corridors. I and my friend helped a little girl, who was only two or three years old, climb up with her father above the water. We were only rescued when people smashed the windows from outside and hauled us out to safety.'

THE HEROES

Many individual acts of heroism were performed that night, not least among them that of Londoner Andrew Parker. In the pitch dark, with a cold black sea rising, carrying with it the wreckage of furniture, old bottles, discarded lifejackets and fuel oil, this brave man turned himself into a human ladder bridging a gap over the water, thus allowing 120 people to clamber over him to safety. He would later be awarded the George Medal for bravery. To this day the nightmare of what happened haunts him and he suffers from post-traumatic stress disorder.

When one man offered himself as a human ladder, more than a hundred people scrambled over him to safety

Another hero was Lieutenant Guido Couwenbergh a Belgian Navy frogman one of the first on the scene. Singlehandedly he saved forty people from drowning. He received the Queen's Gallantry Medal. Couwenbergh and his colleagues

bridge as the *Herald* pulled away from pier 12 at five minutes past six.

Four hundred and thirty-six passengers were on board that night, many of them on the deck watching the twinkling lights of Zeebrugge recede in the distance. In her belly were nearly forty trucks and over eighty cars. For a vessel that could comfortably accommodate a thousand people she was, with her eighty crewmen on top of the passenger complement, marginally over half full.

Barely twenty minutes later the crowded bar, restaurant, duty-free shop, lounges and decks were turned into a maelstrom of nightmare panic as the ship violently listed and then lurched like a giant whale on to her side. It was the start of a night of hell.

As the vessel listed over many passengers were simply sucked out of the windows through sheer force. Larry O'Brian, a lorry driver from Ireland, was sitting in the ship's restaurant when he suddenly saw plates and china fly from the tables. He said: 'In forty-five seconds the boat was on its side and half-filled with water. People were sucked out through portholes like you see in those movies about air disasters. They didn't have a chance. And the boat - well, when I was being taken off it and I

arrived in naval helicopters whose rotors whined noisily above the screams of the trapped and dying below. For them, it was a race against time.

As with the passengers who died in the stricken *Titanic* seventy-five years before them, the cold sea threatened to claim even the strongest swimmer with hypothermia in minutes. One teenager, Nicola Simpson, from Hertfordshire, was clinically dead with a body temperature 25 degrees below normal after she was rescued by Belgian civilian diver Piet Lagast. She was even certified dead on arrival at a Belgian hospital, but thanks to sterling efforts by doctors and nurses who worked throughout the night to raise her temperature, she survived.

Nicola and eight others were trapped behind a sheet of thick glass in the ship that Lagast shattered with his diver's knife - almost severing his hand in the process. He too was a recipient of the Queen's Gallantry Medal.

Massive sodium arc lights were brought to play on the corpse of the doomed vessel as wire reports clattered into TV and newspaper offices around the world. Anguished relatives at Dover docks who besieged the Townsend Thoresen offices attacked pressmen who descended there to cover the worst tragedy in British maritime history in years.

The water was so cold that hospital staff laboured for hours to bring one young girl back from clinical death

---

The Royal Navy was on hand to help in the shape of HMS *Glasgow* and HMS *Diomede,* assisting helicopters from naval squadrons based at Culdrose as they hovered over the living and the dead in the sea. A pilot was later to say: 'I could see black shapes bobbing in the water, arms splayed out like jellyfish and I knew they were the dead.'

THE DOORS THAT NO ONE CLOSED

Daylight brought the real tragedy of Zeebrugge home to the world. Stabilized by tugs, the hulk rested in shallow water on a sandbar with the sea

Below: *A floating crane comes alongside the* **Herald of Free Enterprise.** *Only when righted was the full horror inside revealed.*

Left: *The first articulated truck is lifted from the vehicle deck of the capsized ferry. Many of the dead and injured were lorry drivers.*

Below: *It looked like a wreckers' yard. But these were the cars and trucks of passengers trapped within the freezing, black, waterlogged hulk of the channel ferry.*

coming roughly halfway up her hull. At the front of the ship, plain for all to see and obviously the cause of the disaster, were the cargo deck doors wide open. It was apparent in those hours after the accident that there was an awful lot of explaining to do on someone's behalf.

The captain, David Lewry, as master of his ship, ultimately takes the blame. But the public inquiry which followed proved that the *Herald of Free Enterprise*'s demise rested on far more than one man's shoulders.

It exposed a management system that was out of touch with the day-to-day operations of its fleet and crewmen who were negligent in their duties.

In July 1987, after a twenty-nine-day inquiry, Mr Justice Sheen, who chaired the investigation, concluded that: 'From top to bottom the body was infected by the disease of sloppiness.' Four men, including Captain Lewry, were singled out for making the fatal mistakes which had led to the tragedy. The others were: Senior Master John Kirby, Assistant Boatswain Mark Stanley and Chief Officer Leslie Sabel. Mr Justice Sheen stated plainly what the cause of the accident was.

'The *Herald* sank because she went to sea with her inner and outer bow doors open.' But he went on to say: 'A full investigation into the circumstances of the disaster leads inexorably to the conclusion that the underlying or cardinal faults lay higher up the company.'

It was learned that Mark Stanley, in charge of closing the doors before the ship put to sea, had been asleep at the time. He only woke up as he was thrown from his bunk when the ship keeled over. Leslie Sabel was criticized because he did not check that the doors were shut before sailing. Various captains in the past had expressed concern about the practice of setting sail with the bow doors open to Townsend management in memos. At least one of them expressed the opinion that indicator lights were needed on the bridge to show whether or not bow doors had been closed. The inquiry said that this idea deserved 'serious consideration' - consideration that it had previously not received.

The indirect blame for the tragedy was laid firmly at the feet of sloppy management

---

He went on to say that Captain Lewry ultimately had to carry the burden of responsibility. 'Captain Lewry took the *Herald* to sea with the bow doors fully open. It follows that Captain Lewry must accept personal responsibility for the loss of his ship.' In mitigation it had to be borne in mind, said the judge, that the skipper was working to the same system that existed on other company ships, and that there were no standing orders to close the bow and stern doors.

And he was scathing in his criticism of Townsend's bosses for 'staggering complacency', which led to a 'malaise' which infected it.

After the inquiry, an inquest at Dover ruled that the passengers were the victims of unlawful killing. Charges were later brought against both crewmen and

management, but were later dropped. The memory of what had happened was to be punishment enough.

THE LEGACY

The legacy of the *Herald* disaster was a change in ships' operating procedures. Under maritime law it would be an offence for a vessel to set sail again in a similar fashion.

For the survivors there are only bitter memories left: of loved ones, including Nicola Simpson's mother, who were lost; for crewmen, who saw twelve of their shipmates go down; for Captain Lewry, who in the immediate aftermath of the accident wished he were dead.

The battered and scarred hull of the ship was finally taken apart in a scrapyard in Taiwan.

Above: *Giant floating cranes had to be brought in to raise the* **Herald of Free Enterprise.** *Her battered hulk was later taken apart in a scrapyard in Taiwan.*

ABERFAN SCHOOL
Disaster in the Valleys

The people of coal-mining areas are used to tragedy. But the little village of Aberfan in South Wales was visited by one more terrible than anyone could have imagined when a slagheap engulfed the school and took its children

The story of Wales is written in tragedy. The dark valleys have been witness to much suffering: hardship on the land, poverty in the homes, danger and death in the mines. Above it all, its people have remained strong and proud, descendants of hardy tribes who cherished their Welsh heritage despite its often uncompromising face.

But there is not a man or woman alive who could have foreseen that the greatest tragedy ever to strike Wales would occur in the village of Aberfan - the victim of the mountain that moved to claim the lives of a generation of children. In every sense they were the victims of the

Above: *The close-knit community toiled day and night to recover bodies from their black tomb.*

Opposite: *At 7.30am on 21 October 1966 the mountain of sludge known as Tip No. 7 began to slide towards the village of Aberfan.*

Below: *One of the victims is carried to an ambulance from the buried school.*

pits as much as their fathers and grandfathers - smothered by the very spoil that they had gouged from the earth in order to earn a living.

Aberfan bears the scars of the tragedy to this day, and it is not a village that one can easily feel comfortable in.

The tragedy began at precisely 7.30am on 21 October 1966. Tip no. 7, in National Coal Board parlance, sat like a black cancer on the side of Merthyr Mountain, 500 ft up in the mists and light rain that began to fall as the town stirred for another day. It had rained for weeks, the water acting like a loosening agent on the foul-smelling muck which besmirched the side of the mountain.

At that moment the black slurry began to move, its enormous weight shifting with all the creaks and groans of the beginning of a giant slide. Some 100,000 tons of rocks and mud, hewn by miners from the pits below and around, suddenly began its inexorable journey to the unsuspecting community below.

Little Paul Davies was one of the scabby-kneed kids of Aberfan who was in the Pantglas infants' and junior school at the foot of the mountain - one of a cluster of buildings that included a row of cottages and a farm. Five-year-old Paul loved drawing, and was sketching even as the unstoppable slurry was gathering momentum, moving faster and faster for its appointment with catastrophe. He drew clockfaces, all of them saying 9.25. One picture showed a mountain of sludge

Above: *Rescue workers dig among the rubble after the rain-soaked coal tip avalanched onto the infants' school.*

Right: *Prince Philip, Duke of Edinburgh, rushed to the scene to talk to rescue workers and comfort relatives of the dead.*

sliding onto his school while a plane marked 'National Coal Board' dropped bombs on to the mountain.

At 9.25am the moving mountain hit Pantglas infants' school. Later, when they pulled little Paul's smothered body from underneath the school clock, it was stuck at 9.25.

The tide of sludge had hit with the force of a hurricane, smothering, smashing, crushing everything in its path.

Survivors recall hearing the screech of dragged gravel and breaking rocks reaching a crescendo shortly before it broke over the village below.

THE TERRIBLE DEATH TOLL

The Rev. Kenneth Hayes remembers those split seconds with awful clarity. It is a moment in time that will never leave him. He rounded the corner of a street to see a mound of slurry climbing up the outside of the school building before the sheer weight behind it pushed it through on its lethal mission. His nine-year-old son Dyfig was among those it claimed.

'The slurry just overwhelmed the school,' he said. 'I saw the last of the living being taken out and the first of the dead. I knew I had lost my boy, although his body was not found until the following day. That was when the enormity of it all dawned on us. Whole families had been wiped out. I buried five from one house that Thursday.'

Phillip Thomas remembers crying as the stones crushed his hands, and calling out desperately for his 'mam'. He had left the school on an errand with another boy, and so was out of the classroom when the wall of mud smashed into it. He recalled:

I was buried immediately and found myself crying. Then all I remember was men digging me out, and muddy water was pouring, pouring all over me. Robert, the boy on the errand, was found two days later - dead. My right hand was crushed so badly I lost three fingers. My leg was injured, my pelvis fractured, my hair gone. I had bleeding internally and externally and they said I would have bled to death if the mud hadn't caked on me, forming a skin. The force of the mud was such that it smashed my spleen, which had to be removed, and ripped off an ear, which had to be sewn back on.

One boy would have bled to death if the mud had not formed a protective cake over his injuries

Susan Maybank, nearly eight years old, was sitting in her classroom. Her teacher glanced out of the window just as he saw the merciless black monster

about to engulf the school, and shouted a warning for her and her classmates to dive under their desks.

Seconds later, as the children - some of them believing they were playing an exciting new game - were on all fours, the slurry smashed through the walls as if they were paper. The teacher died instantly, and Susan remembers being engulfed by the cold blackness.

She has no idea how long she was underground - all she remembers was pushing her fingers through the muck to form an air-hole and waving them around. The small army of men - pensioners, off-duty miners, policemen, firemen, builders, doctors, solicitors, bakers and cooks - that had descended on the school to begin frantically clawing at the rubble with their bare hands rescued her. In the slime were her best friends, entombed forever.

Eye-witnesses to the tragedy will never forget the scene of the sweating, wet-eyed men, their limbs trembling with rage and fury, their hands bleeding.

Elizabeth Jones was trapped for several hours with the dead body of another child jammed up against her. Now aged thirty-one, she believes she

Above: *Bereaved families weep at the communal grave where eighty tiny coffins were laid to rest side by side.*

Right: *A shocked world reacted immediately to the disaster by sending thousands of consoling letters containing hard-earned cash and cheques for the Aberfan Disaster Fund.*

escaped because she left a classroom to take her dinner money along to the school office when it happened.

'I only remember being engulfed in masonry and sludge,' she said.

I was trapped in the school corridor for a long time with the body of a little boy beneath me and by the side of me. When they pulled me out I was still holding my shilling dinner money. I am sure that saved me and I still keep it as a lucky coin.

Another souvenir is the plaster cast which my leg was in for months afterwards. Most of my memories have mercifully faded - when your mind luckily begins to think of other things. But I received severe internal injuries in the slide and as a result will never be able to have children.

All day and into the night the frantic struggle for survivors went on. Lord Snowdon and the ashen-faced Secretary of State for Wales, George Thomas, arrived to see the pathetic bodies of the children being plucked one by one from the black sea.

Later the agony was too much even for hardened journalists to bear as the children's pathetic corpses were laid in the Morriah Chapel for their agonized parents to come and identify them. An anguished keening rose into the skies above Aberfan that day: 'Why us, oh Lord, why us?'

By nightfall the generators hummed as the sodium arc lamps threw their light on the shattered school and surrounding buildings. Still the remains of tip no. 7 continued to yield casualties up from its smothering clutches.

Bryn Carpenter was in hospital the morning of the slide, recovering from a pit accident himself. He was rushed to the scene and found a sight more terrifying than anything he had ever witnessed below ground. He said:

We believed our ten-year-old Desmond was buried in there. When they told us of an unidentified ten-year-old in hospital our spirits lifted, but it turned out to be someone else.

Later that night they found Desmond's body. We were by no means alone in our grief. In my street alone we lost fourteen. Two houses lost two children each. And time doesn't heal - there is always something there to trigger grief again.

One of the lucky ones was Pat Lewis, whose eldest sister Sharon was killed in the slime that she managed to escape from. Just a week shy of her ninth birthday, she saw the wall splitting behind the teacher as he stood up to call the names on the morning register. Her shouted warning enabled him to get many of the children outside, and she was saved.

Her mother, Sheila, scooped her in her arms as she arrived home - apologizing because her coat was still in the school. Sheila, a trained nurse, went back with her to the school and climbed in through a broken window. She recalled:

Inside were about twenty children who had been swept forward by the fast-approaching tip as it bulldozed the building. They were the ones who could be helped, though one of those children walked out of the ruins, seemingly all right, then collapsed and died.

I laid the survivors on blankets in the school yard and turned the infants' classroom into a first aid post. I worked the whole day but nobody came out alive after 11am. It was the most horrifying day, but your senses sharpen at times like that and so I can remember it all clearly.

I knew I couldn't go and identify Sharon's body. My poor husband had to go and do it. He came back from the chapel at about 5am on Saturday and

Below: *Homes too were destroyed as the killer coal slagheap swept past the infants' school and engulfed part of the village.*

Above: *A touching tribute to the eighty children who perished. This giant Cross of Aberfan was made out of wreaths and flowers on a hillside overlooking the cemetery.*

Left: *Villagers openly wept as they witnessed bodies being brought out of the rubble and mud that was once a village school.*

said he recognized her. She had been found with the rest of the class and the teacher. I was sitting on a stool by the fire and I remember I slid back against the wall and made a terrible noise for I don't know how long.

Body after tiny body was laid in the chapel, their eyes and mouths filled with coal slurry that parents angrily cleaned out so their loved ones could rest with dignity. Throughout the night the parents came, and Aberfan was plunged into the post-shock trauma of a town that had suffered and lost on a tremendous scale. The final tally of dead was 144. Of the 116 schoolchildren, most of them were under the age of ten.

Afterwards, of course, bureaucrats moved in for the biggest government inquiry ever held. It lasted five months, and heard evidence from 136 witnesses.

Controversially the Coal Board chairman Alfred Robens, later Lord Robens, stayed away - although he attended later as the community felt painfully snubbed by his absence.

Due to goodness knows what rules of accounting, the government paid out £500 to each family that had lost a child. A further £5000 went to each family from a special fund patronized by the Queen, Prince Philip and Prince Charles.

THE TRAGEDY THAT SHOULD NEVER HAVE HAPPENED

There was only one verdict - that it could have all been prevented.

It emerged that there was no national safety policy for tips like Aberfan. The Coal Board was held to be legally liable for what had happened when it emerged that mandarins in the industry had ignored warnings about the dangerous state of the Aberfan tip since as far back as 1960.

Warnings about the state of the tip at Aberfan had been ignored for the previous six years.

Lord Robens had to live with the memory of what had happened to Aberfan, with the knowledge that it need never have occurred. In 1986, when newspapers around the world ran a retrospective on the tragedy to mark its twentieth anniversary, he said:

The one question I constantly turn over in my mind is how it could have been prevented. There were thousands of pit heaps all over the country and they all came within the local pit authority's guidelines. It is awful that it takes something like that to make sure every safety regulation is double-checked and brought into practice.

When I think of all I did during my time with the Coal Board it diminishes to nothing when I think of the Aberfan disaster. It is a terrible thing which will always haunt me.

On the bleak hillside above Aberfan stands one of the most poignant sights in Britain - row upon row of children's gravestones, the victims of the moving mountain that claimed them that day.

MI5 SPY RING
A Web of Deception

The sensational defection of Burgess and Maclean in 1951 triggered the exposure of a web of espionage and double dealing. For decades Englishmen in high places had been spying for the Russians

It was in the unlikely surroundings of Cambridge University that the twentieth century's most dangerous spy ring was spawned. In the 1930s as ex-public schoolboys punted down the River Cam, they formed the idea that Communism provided a better life and a stronger way to fight Fascism.

A former Russian envoy to London had started the recruitment ball rolling. Maxim Litvinov theorized that these undergraduates, already on the lower rungs of the Establishment ladder, would never have their loyalty doubted. So the Russian net was cast.

And within just a few years it hauled in a group of Cambridge students. Guy Burgess, Donald Maclean, Anthony Blunt and Kim Philby were to cause untold damage to Britain. Many died because of their treachery. Yet none of the spies was ever brought to justice.

In the thirties many undergraduates turned to Communism as a way of rejecting Fascism

---

It was Blunt who led the way to Cambridge and to Trinity College, which was to have the dubious distinction of being the breeding ground for each of the traitors. The son of a vicar, brilliant and a homosexual, he arrived at Trinity in 1928. He was a gifted student in mathematics, languages and art, and after he graduated he became a teaching Fellow.

Above: *Anthony Blunt's shame as a Soviet spy went unrevealed for years. He continued in his post as adviser to the Queen on her fabulous art collection.*

Opposite: *Kim Philby holds a press conference after he was wrongly cleared of being the 'Third Man' in the Burgess-Maclean affair.*

Right: *Foreign office intelligence chief Donald Maclean in a conference with the then British Ambassador to Washington, Sir John Balfour.*

Harold Philby - nicknamed Kim - arrived in 1929. And a year later they were joined by old Etonian Guy Francis de Moncy Burgess, an eccentric homosexual with a large capacity for alcohol and indiscreet gossip. Donald Maclean, the son of a religious Liberal cabinet minister, arrived in 1931.

Many Trinity College students became Communists. But for most it was a passing phase. For these four it became their life's work.

After university Maclean went to the Foreign Office. One of his interviewers,

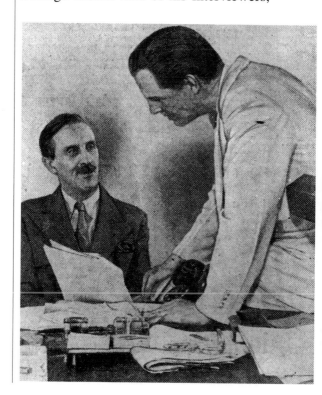

he later said, asked him: 'We understand that you held strong Communist views while you were at Cambridge. Do you still hold those views?'

'I decided to brazen it out. "Yes," I said "I did have such views - and I haven't entirely shaken them off." They must have liked my honesty.'

After Trinity, Burgess talked his way into a job with Tory MP Jack Macnamara. Burgess had already visited Russia and had met spy chiefs to arrange his contacts in London. He and Blunt became the organizers of the spy ring.

He was making contacts all the time and as war approached he became a secret courier carrying messages to European leaders. All the information he gained he was passing back to his Soviet spymasters. But at the same time he was feeding tip-offs to British Intelligence. His devious hard work paid off. In January 1939 MI6 offered him a staff job.

After Cambridge Philby went to Vienna, where he helped Communists to escape from the Nazis. He reappeared in London with a wife – a Soviet spy – and began to cultivate a right-wing image. In 1937 he went to Spain to cover the Civil War for the *Times* as a reporter. It was a useful cover to feed back information to the Russians, who were supporting the Republicans.

WAR WORK

In 1939 Blunt applied for a five-week military intelligence course. His Marxist past caught up with him, and he was returned to his unit as a 'security risk'.

But he wasn't downhearted by his first failure to infiltrate the security services. He joined the Army's Intelligence Corps and was evacuated from Dunkirk. And then, via the 'old boy' network, he was recruited by MI5.

Philby's chance to infiltrate the Secret Services came with a surprise phone call in June 1940 from the War Office. He was offered a job in Section D, in a new department formed to cause subversive chaos in Europe. His interviewers for the job included one Guy Burgess! And he soon progressed into MI6.

The job of MI5 was to protect security at home, while MI6 was in charge of

Right: *Donald Maclean in characteristic pose. This was the elegant Englishman who traded life in the West for a mundane existence behind the Iron Curtain.*

Opposite: *'Fourth Man' Anthony Blunt with the three defectors from British intelligence in the fifties and sixties - Guy Burgess, Donald Maclean and Kim Philby.*

Below: *A gardener tends the grounds of Maclean's house in Tatsfield, Kent, while the hunt goes on for the missing diplomat.*

intelligence-gathering abroad. Already Guy Burgess was hard at work for his Russian bosses.

Soviet Embassy cipher clerks were working full-time to encode the mass of material for transmission to Moscow.

Philby started by sending lists of agents, codenames and wavelengths from the central archives of the Secret Intelligence Services.

And from inside MI5 Blunt made sure that Russian atom spies Dr Klaus Fuchs and Dr Alan Nunn May could continue their work on the atom bomb – despite their obvious Communist leanings.

Above: *Maclean sent telegrams from Paris in 1951. To his mother he said: 'Am quite all right.' To his wife he said: 'Don't stop loving me.'*

Left: *Guy Burgess's mother, Mrs Jack Bassett in 1956.*

Below: *Guy Burgess (left)* with **Daily Express** *man Terence Lancaster in Moscow in 1957.*

At the same time as supporting these two scientists Blunt was accepting a new job - as Surveyor of the King's Pictures. His disloyalty knew no bounds.

In 1944 Maclean was appointed Head of Chancery at the British Embassy in Washington. One of his first calls was to the Soviet Consulate to meet his new controller.

He would have a lot of information to give him. Memos between Roosevelt and Churchill outlining war plans and post-war policy crossed his desk. And then after World War II Maclean was made secretary of the committee that dealt as the clearing house for atomic bomb information between the Western allies.

Meanwhile Philby had been promoted to a plum job too. He was made head of Section Nine, the department controlling espionage against Russia. It meant that Russia was warned of every planned spying mission against them.

RUMOURS AND DANGERS

The sheer bulk of information that the four were providing meant that suspicions were bound to be aroused. It was the Americans who first asked: why do the Russians know everything we're doing, before we've done it?

There was one specific case that threatened to uncover Philby. In August 1945 the Secret Service received a message that KGB man Konstantin Volkov wanted to defect to Britain with his wife. In return he promised to reveal the name of three British spies working for the Soviets in the Foreign Office and the Secret Service. Luckily for Philby, he was given the case to handle personally.

When a Russian defector offered to unmask British moles, it was Philby who was put in charge of the case!

When Philby arrived in Turkey, where he was supposed to meet the Russian, Volkov did not appear. He was next seen in Moscow – with a bullet in the back of his head. Years later the cynical Philby explained: 'It was either Volkov's head or mine.' And despite US suspicions, he got away with it.

After the war Burgess entered the

Foreign Office and became personal assistant to Hector MacNeil, the Labour government's deputy Foreign Secretary.

But the strain was telling on Burgess and Maclean and they were turning to drink. Maclean was sent to Cairo. But it didn't stop his boozing. After a drunken rampage, during which he snatched a nightwatchman's gun and then broke his leg, he was sent back to Britain.

By 1950 Burgess was in a terrible state. An official report on him stated: 'The sooner we get rid of this appalling man the better for all of us.' Wherever he went, he engaged in drinking bouts and fights. He launched vicious attacks on British policy. Still in August 1950 he was posted to Washington as first secretary. There he joined Philby, who had been appointed MI6's liaison man with the CIA.

But the noose around the spy ring's neck was tightening. Philby had already warned Burgess that British security was closing in on Foreign Office suspects.

In Washington he took Burgess under his wing - and under his roof. It was his last chance, the Foreign Office had decided. But both Burgess and Philby were still passing useful information to the Russians in Washington.

ESCAPE TO THE EAST

By 1951 Philby knew, because of his privileged position, that Maclean was close to being exposed. What he did not know was that the Americans had also targeted him and Burgess.

Maclean had to be warned, and had to escape. If he was captured he was bound to talk - he had become a nervous wreck. Philby nominated Burgess as messenger, but he could not return to Britain without an official reason. He contrived a series of embarrassing incidents, so the Ambassador had to order him home.

It was Blunt who discovered from his MI5 contacts the exact time when 'Homer' - the mole's codename - was to be picked up. On 25 May 1951 Foreign Secretary Herbert Morrison signed the paper ordering Maclean's interrogation.

Burgess knew within minutes and contacted Maclean. On the pretext of taking a holiday, they boarded a ferry to

Above: *Donald Maclean's wife Melinda arrives back from France with her family after the disappearance of her husband.*

Left: *The Maclean family car was found eight days after his disappearance, in a Lausanne garage.*

France that night. Neither was to be seen in Britain again. Their next public appearance was in 1956, when they were paraded in Moscow as heroes of the Communist struggle.

Why Burgess joined Maclean in his flight has never been revealed. He probably panicked. Their hurried flight left the remaining two Cambridge spies to face the music.

THE CHARMED LIFE OF A TRAITOR

It took a matter of hours for the authorities to link Philby with Burgess and Maclean's sudden disappearance. He was summoned back to London by MI6 chief Sir Stewart Menzies. Somehow Philby brazened it out, putting the blame

At Cambridge we had both been communists. We abandoned our political activities not because we disagreed with the Marxist analysis of the world situation, in which we still all find ourselves, but because we thought, wrongly it is now clear to us, that in the public service we could do more to put these ideas into practical effect than elsewhere.

It is probably our action in necessarily giving up political activities by entering the public service that, falsely analysed the Foreign Office to say through its spokesman that it "believed" we had been Soviet agents at Cambridge. The Foreign Office can of course "believe" anything it wishes. The important point however is that on this question we know, and it does not We neither of us have ever been communist agents.

So far the ground was common for us both. The details of our subsequent careers were completely different and had therefore better be dealt with separately.

As regards Maclean, he worked in London and in Paris, Washington and Cairo as a regular member of the Foreign Service

Above: *The signed thousand-word statement of Burgess and Maclean. In it they say: 'Neither of us have ever been Communist agents.'*

fairly and squarely on the now absent Burgess. Philby was allowed to resign and take a £4000 golden handshake.

In his wake he left chaos. Ten intelligence service officials were forced to resign - not for being moles, but for failing to prevent spying.

In 1955 the government published the long-awaited White Paper on the disappearance of Burgess and Maclean. It was a whitewash. One MP described it as 'an insult to the intelligence of the country'.

But the most dangerous moment came for Philby when MP Marcus Lipton tabled a parliamentary question. The MP, primed by MI5, asked Tory Prime Minister Sir Anthony Eden: 'Have you made up your mind to cover up at all costs the dubious third man activities of Harold Philby?'

In 1955 Philby was named as the Third Man. Despite government warnings, MI6 continued to use him as an agent

---

For the first time Philby had been named as the so-called Third Man. And because the question was covered by parliamentary privilege the press could report it without running the risk of libel.

Foreign Secretary Harold Macmillan answered the question and told the House the conclusions of the Foreign Service's investigations:

I have no reason to conclude that Mr

Philby has at any time betrayed the interests of this country, or to identify him with the so-called 'Third Man', if indeed there was one....

Philby was cock-a-hoop and held a press conference to celebrate. 'I have never been a Communist,' he lied.

MI6 took all this as a cue to use Philby as an agent again, when he was in the Middle East as a reporter for the *Observer* newspaper. There he began to feed the Soviets information again.

THE NET CLOSES

But Philby could not escape the truth for ever. MI5 still insisted that Philby was a mole, and final proof came with the sudden defection of Russian KGB man Anatoli Golitsin. He identified Philby as the Third Man beyond doubt.

In January 1963 agent Nicholas Elliott, an old friend of Philby's, flew to confront him with the new evidence.

'You took me in for years,' he said. 'Now I'll get the truth out of you even if I have to drag it out. I once looked up to you, Kim. God, how I despise you now.'

The Attorney-General, Sir John Hobson, had agreed that the spy could be offered immunity from prosecution - in exchange for a full confession.

He revealed how he had been recruited and trained, and detailed his work as a double agent. But he refused to name his contacts and to sign a written confession.

As Elliott returned to England for further instructions, Philby fled. In July the Supreme Soviet granted Philby's request for political asylum. Not only that, they gave him Russian citizenship and a job in the KGB as well!

Right: *Mrs Philby and a journalist in Beirut. She had reported her husband's disappearance but then heard that he had fled to Moscow.*

THE MOLE AT THE PALACE

His escape left only the aesthetic intellectual Anthony Blunt still in place. Blunt had worked closely with Burgess, and now he feared that he would blurt out the truth from the safety of Moscow - to where Blunt had refused to flee.

By the time that Blunt faced William Skardon, the ace interrogator, he had already been questioned eleven times. This time though, he was faced with harder evidence. After being offered immunity, and after pouring himself a stiff drink, he then poured out his entire confession.

But astonishingly, despite his confession, the spy was allowed to keep his job as Surveyor of the Queen's Pictures and often met her in the course of his duties.

It was not until fourteen years later that Premier Margaret Thatcher was forced to act when the truth was uncovered by author Andrew Boyle. She announced: 'In April 1964, Sir Anthony Blunt admitted to the security authorities that he had passed information regularly to the Russians when he was a member of the Security Services...'

Minutes later Buckingham Palace announced that Blunt had been stripped of his knighthood.

The Queen was informed that her art advisor was a self-confessed spy

---

The so-called Mole at the Palace was finally exposed. He died disgraced seven years later, unloved save by his long-term homosexual partner, John Gaskin. At his funeral Blunt's brother Christopher said 'Anthony bitterly regretted that he got it wrong. But he was not ashamed. He was on the tiger and could not get off.' Burgess had died earlier, in 1963, homesick and an alcoholic. Maclean died in the same month as Blunt. Philby continued working for the KGB until the very end.

He swore that the only things he missed about Britain were the cricket scores and marmalade. But in 1982 a Russian freighter was spotted moored off the Sussex coast. On the bridge with a pair of binoculars was a stooped figure. It was Philby, taking a last longing look.

He died in Moscow in May 1988 and was given a full military send-off in Moscow's Kuntsevo cemetery.

Above: *Kim Philby with his mother in November 1955.*

Below: *Anthony Blunt addresses a press conference in London in 1980. He tried to fudge the accusations that he was the long-sought 'Fourth Man' in Britain's worst espionage ring.*

TENERIFE
Take-off to Tragedy

On a foggy day in 1977 two jumbos were diverted to a small, single-runway airport in the Canaries. As a result nearly six hundred people died in the worst airline disaster the world has ever known

Pan American pilot Victor Grubbs carefully taxied his fully loaded 747 along the runway at Los Rodeos airport, waiting for the all-clear for take-off. But as he steered the giant craft down the runway, he could scarcely believe what he saw through the cockpit window. Some 350 yards away he saw the lights of another 747, owned by the Dutch airline KLM, emerge from the fog.

At first, both Captain Grubbs and his flight crew thought the other plane was parked, but as the lights drew brighter it became terrifyingly clear that the Dutch jumbo was heading straight for them at 160 mph.

'We are still on the runway!' Grubbs screamed to the air traffic controllers in the tower. 'What's he doing? He'll kill us all!' His co-pilot, Robert Bragg, yelled for him to 'Get off! Get off!'

Desperately, Captain Grubbs swerved sharply to the left, heading for the grassy shoulder just off the runway. Tragically, he was a few seconds too late, as the KLM liner crashed broadside into the Pan Am clipper. Within seconds, the airstrip became a mass of tangled metal,

Above: *The arid peaks whose height causes the thick fogs that so often blank out Tenerife's airspace.*

Opposite: *The tailplane of the Pan Am jumbo jet after the worst air disaster in history.*

Below: *Tenerife is a sunny haunt for holidaymakers and the business heart of the Canary Islands.*

exploding fuel tanks and burning flesh.

It was 27 March 1977 - a day that saw the death of 583 Dutch and American citizens in the worst aviation disaster that had ever taken place.

BITTER IRONY

The tragedy was filled with the most bitter of ironies: neither plane had even intended stopping at Los Rodeos, a second-rate airport that was never considered among the safest in the region. But a terrorist bomb had exploded at their original destination, the more modern facility at Las Palmas some 70 miles away, and for safety's sake both aircraft had been rerouted to Tenerife.

That day had begun in a mood of innocent good humour. The Dutch airliner was carrying 283 holidaymakers, eager to begin their Easter break on Las Palmas.

The Pan Am clipper was carrying 380 passengers to a rendezvous with the cruise ship *Golden Odyssey*.

The disaster would never have happened if Las Palmas airport had not been closed due to a terrorist bomb

---

The re-routing seemed no more than a minor inconvenience, and both jumbos landed without incident. Captain Grubbs taxied his clipper, Victor, up to the terminal building and parked it alongside another 747, the Rhine, skippered by Captain Jacob Louis Veldhuyzen van Zanten, KLM's chief jumbo instructor.

Once the Rhine had been refuelled, Captain Veldhuyzen van Zanten asked for flight clearance. According to aviation officials, at Los Rodeos a plane would normally taxi its way to the south-east corner of the field for take-off, but because of the emergency at Las Palmas that route was now crowded by other diverted planes. So the tower instructed the KLM plane to taxi up the runway itself, and at the end Veldhuyzen van Zanten made a 180-degree turn and prepared for take-off.

At the same time, the tower instructed Grubbs too to taxi up the runway, but told him to turn off by the third exit on his left, thus leaving the airstrip free for the

KLM jumbo. A few minutes later, controllers asked him if he had made the turn. When Grubbs replied that he hadn't, they told him: 'Do it, and advise when the runway is clear.'

But as the clipper continued up the runway, shrouded in mist and therefore invisible both to the Dutch plane and to the tower, the KLM crew made its last transmission to the tower: 'KLM....We are now ready on [or 'at' - the exact wording was garbled] take-off.'

Grubbs's worst nightmare was happening. The KLM was hurtling out of the fog at 160 mph, and heading straight for him. Frantically he radioed the tower

Above: *The burnt-out skeleton of the tail section of Pan Am's jumbo jet on the runway of Santa Cruz airport.*

that he was still on the runway, then swore angrily as he desperately gunned his engines and jerked his plane to the left. As he did so, Veldhuyzen van Zanten urgently tried to take his plane into the air. Its nose lifted but the tail remained on the runway, digging an ugly, gaping trench.

IMPACT

It smashed into the Pan Am jumbo in the forward part of the second-class section, while its right wing slashed through the bubble atop the cockpit, slicing off the roof. The Pan Am clipper, cut in half and already on fire, toppled to the side of the runway.

A split second later, the Dutch plane slammed back to the ground, skidded around backwards and screeched to a halt about 300 yards away. In an instant, it exploded into a ball of flames, the inferno gorging itself on its just-filled fuel tanks. Everyone on board was killed. The impact was so hard and the explosive fire so hot that aluminium and steel parts on both planes were vaporized.

Back on board the American plane, there was pandemonium. Debris seemed to be falling from everywhere, and the flames were quickly spreading. Terrified and dazed, those who could scrambled to get out. Many were already dead, and

Above: *The passengers who packed the Dutch and American jumbos had dreamed of lazing on sun-drenched beaches fanned by Atlantic breezes.*

La Candelaria Hospital began dealing with the wounded. Most of them had rushed to the hospital as word spread of the crash, and they worked gallantly under the most difficult conditions.

There were not enough beds for all the dying and the injured, so orderlies laid them on the floor while nurses scampered about handing out painkillers and sedatives and doctors began the task of stripping away burned skin.

Other survivors who had less serious injuries were huddled in the airport terminal. Blankets and painkillers were handed out to the stunned passengers, some of whom had had the clothes burned off their backs. Each of them spoke of their escape as miraculous. 'I felt someone was watching over me,' said Theresa Brusco. 'It was like we had a guardian angel around us.'

WHAT WENT WRONG?

By this stage, scores of soldiers and police were combing through the gutted wreckage of both planes, engaged in the grisly task of sorting out bodies.

What had gone wrong? A horde of aviation experts from the United States, Holland and Spain quickly descended on Los Rodeos to find out, and at first suspicion fell on the air traffic controllers. It had been rumoured that they did not speak very good English - the language of international air traffic control - and that the two pilots might have been confused.

But that was quickly dispelled when investigators interviewed the three men who had been in the tower at the time of the crash. They all spoke 'textbook' English, and had followed take-off procedures to the letter.

The probe then targeted the captains, Grubbs and Veldhuyzen van Zanten.

At first, Dutch experts challenged the American flyer's conduct over the question of runway exits. There were four such exits along the runway, marked C-1 to C-4. KLM officials argued that Grubbs had been ordered to turn off at C-3 and that, had he done so, the catastrophe would never have occurred.

But Pan Am countered by claiming that their pilot had merely been told to

others were too stunned to move.

Inside the twisted wreck, heroic thirty-three-year-old businessman Edgar Ridout tried to organize an evacuation.

Some of the Pan Am passengers were in such shock that they just stood there as if nothing had happened

---

The brave businessman helped one of the stewardesses inflate a life raft so that passengers could jump onto it as they leaped from the plane.

HEROES AND SURVIVORS

There were many heroes that day. As burning debris and red-hot metal continued to shower the immediate area, melting the runway, Jack Daniel helped his wife and daughter to safety, then disappeared. His frightened wife began frantically asking if anyone had seen a man in a white suit. Someone answered that he had heard a woman screaming for help, and that a man in a white suit had raced back to help. Then there was another explosion, and both had disappeared.

Meanwhile, as the tragedy continued to unfold, doctors and nurses at the nearby

THE VERDICT

It took an exhaustive, eighteen-month investigation before the Spanish government would release its findings.

The tragic verdict of the investigation was that Captain Veldhuyzen van Zanten had decided to start his take-off run without clearance, and that had been 'the fundamental cause'.

The report recalled that the weather was dismal that day, with low-scudding clouds and fog that sharply reduced visibility. But that on its own couldn't account for the Dutchman's strange and inexplicable decision.

How could a veteran pilot like Veldhuyzen van Zanten have made such an incredible mistake? It seems that, harried by an already lengthy delay on Tenerife and the erratic weather conditions, he may have rushed his take-off to avoid violating a KLM rule against crew overtime.

The radio 'whistle' could have beeped out some essential communications. And imprecise language used by both the tower and the KLM crew may have confused matters still further.

In the end, to those who died, it didn't matter...because just seconds later, the world's worst-ever aviation disaster occurred.

take 'the third exit' on the left. Pan Am executive William Waltrip asserted that C-1 was 'inactive', and that C-3 would have required an extremely difficult turn of 150 degrees. Therefore, the Americans maintained, the logical 'third exit' was C-4 - the one Grubbs never reached.

Moreover, argued the Americans, no matter where the clipper was supposed to be, Veldhuyzen van Zanten should never have taken off without clearance from the tower. The head of the Dutch investigation team had shocked his countrymen when he stated that he had found no clearance for the KLM take-off on the tower's nine-minute audio tape.

Top: *A memorial service for the victims of the disaster was conducted at Schiphol Airport, Amsterdam. On the runway were 232 coffins decked with flowers.*

Above: *Mourners leave the memorial service at Schiphol Airport.*

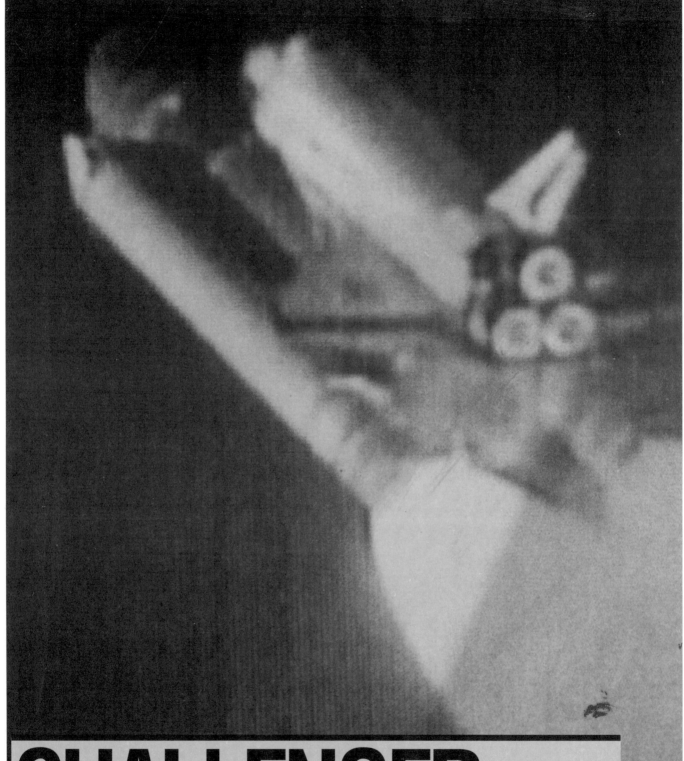

CHALLENGER
A Shattered Dream

In January 1986 a fireball of horror erupted into the sunny Florida skies. After twenty-five successful missions the Challenger space shuttle had blown up, killing all aboard her. What went wrong? And why were the warnings ignored?

The morning of 28 January 1986 began like many others for the skilled team of NASA scientists and engineers at Cape Canaveral, as they checked and rechecked the Space Shuttle *Challenger* in preparation for what they thought would be another routine mission in space for the reusable craft.

The seven astronauts - including Christa McAuliffe, who was to be the first civilian in space - were given last-minute briefings and instructions. And around the massive base, thousands of excited spectators and media representatives had gathered to await the spectacular launch.

None could have known that within seconds of that spectacular lift-off, the unthinkable would happen. The *Challenger* would explode in a fiery orange-and-white ball, killing all the crew members aboard and derailing the American space programme for almost three years.

In one tragic instant, the world's complacency towards manned space flight would evaporate forever nine miles up in the blue skies over Florida.

One spectator's scream was heard and repeated around the world: 'Oh, my God! What's happened?'

Opposite: *A moment of hope as* **Challenger** *takes to the skies. Within seconds came disaster.*

Below: *The* **Challenger***'s astronauts line up for the photo album before take-off from Cape Canaveral on 28 January 1986.*

PRELUDE TO TRAGEDY

The story of *Challenger*'s fateful trip to oblivion began the previous night, as temperatures in the normally temperate Florida winter plunged to an unseasonable 27 degrees.

A spectator screamed: 'Oh, my God! What's happened?' Her agonized cry was heard by millions on TV worldwide

---

Early the next morning, NASA's so-called 'ice team' went to work, inspecting the shuttle for any signs of potentially dangerous build-ups of ice which could break away on lift-off and harm the *Challenger*'s heat-shield tiles.

It would later emerge that an engineer working with the Rockwell company in California, who had been watching the inspection on closed circuit television, called mission control to urge a delay because of the ice.

The gathered masses who stood cheering the astronauts as they walked to the *Challenger*, veteran of nine previous flights, knew nothing of the frantic warning which had come from three thousand miles away. Nor did the crew.

Once on board, they began their detailed checks of all systems with the aid of the craft's main computer.

Everything seemed right for the mission which included the deployment of a $100 million communications satellite into space and several on-board experiments. The astronauts were to measure the spectrum of Halley's comet; to sample radiation within the spacecraft at various points; and to examine the effects of weightlessness on the development of twelve chicken embryos.

From three thousand miles away came the unheeded advice to delay the launch because of the cold weather

---

At T minus seven minutes and thirty seconds the walkway was finally pulled away from the billion-dollar shuttle and its three huge engines.

The external tank stood more than ten storeys high and carried more than half a

Above: *The space shuttle lifts off from launch pad 39B. The orbiter craft carried the doomed crew of seven.*

million gallons of liquid oxygen and liquid hydrogen. The two booster rockets were packed with more than one million pounds of solid fuel.

The public address system continued: 'T minus forty-five seconds and counting,' as those in the huge crowd talked excitedly among themselves.

On board, Commander Dick Scobee and Pilot Michael Smith were strapped into the flight deck. Directly behind them were Judith Resnik, an electrical engineer, and Ronald McNair, a physicist. On the mid-deck below were Ellison Onizuka, an aerospace engineer,

Gregory Jarvis, an electrical engineer, and Christa McAuliffe.

With six seconds to go, the main engine was started. The roar was deafening.

'Four...three...two...one...and lift-off. Lift-off of the twenty-fifth space shuttle mission. And it has cleared the tower.' The spectators began to cheer wildly for the spectacular rise to the heavens.

Among those who watched the *Challenger*'s graceful ascent, its white plume of smoke shining brilliantly behind, were McAuliffe's family and eighteen of her third-grade class who had travelled some fifteen hundred miles from Concord, New Hampshire to see their teacher make history.

Sixteen seconds after launch the huge craft turned gracefully on its back as the main fuel tank and the two booster rockets assumed the course for leaving the earth's atmosphere. Mission control pronounced that all three engines were running smoothly.

'*Challenger*, go with throttle up,' said mission control exactly fifty-two seconds after launch. 'Roger, go with throttle up,' Scobee radioed back.

Three seconds later, NASA's long-range television cameras picked up an appallingly unfamiliar sight.

Television viewers could see what those below could not. A tiny but distinct orange glow flashed near the middle of the shuttle, between its underside and the external tank.

A split second later, the unthinkable nightmare happened. The *Challenger* was momentarily engulfed in flames, then disintegrated.

Unaware of the explosion, the official announcer continued his narration while the incredulous spectators watched in horror

---

Spectators felt an unspeakable horror as the hideous Y-shaped cloud spewed above them.

Incredibly, back at mission control in Houston, the official announcer had not been watching the TV monitor. Instead, he had his eyes glued on the programmed flight data displayed in front of him, and

reported what should have been the readings from *Challenger*.

'One minute, fifteen seconds. Velocity 2900 feet per second. Altitude nine nautical miles. Downrange distance seven nautical miles.' To the stunned millions watching on television, the narration was surreal.

Suddenly, he stopped. A minute later he announced: 'We have a report from the flight dynamics officer that the vehicle has exploded. The flight director confirms that.'

In Washington, President Ronald Reagan was working in the Oval Office when suddenly his top aides burst in.

'There's been a serious incident with the space shuttle,' said Vice President George Bush. Patrick Buchanan, the White House Communications Director, was much more blunt: 'Sir, the shuttle has exploded.'

Reagan, like the rest of America, was stunned. It was his decision that the first private citizen in space should be a schoolteacher. McAuliffe had been selected from more than eleven thousand hopeful applicants.

Below: *The view from Kennedy Space Center as* **Challenger** *explodes within moments of its launch.*

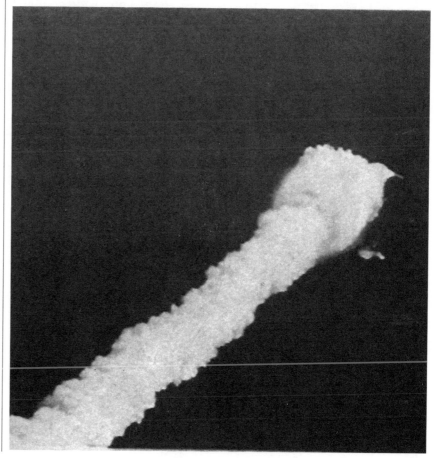

A few hours later he would try to soothe a grieving nation with a poignant speech in which he said that the seven pioneers had 'left the surly bonds of earth to touch the face of God'.

Then, addressing the nation's schoolchildren Reagan added: 'I know it's hard to understand that sometimes painful things like this happen. It's all part of the process of exploration...and expanding man's horizons.'

GRIEF AND SORROW

Americans were shaken. Their scientists and astronauts had soared into space fifty-five times over the past quarter of a century, and their safe return had come to be taken for granted. An age when almost anyone, given a few months' training, could go along for a safe ride seemed at hand. McAuliffe, a vivacious high school teacher, was to be the standard bearer of that new era. Tragically, the era lasted just seventy-three seconds.

'They have left the surly bonds of earth to touch the face of God,' said President Reagan in a moving speech

---

After undergoing rigorous training for three months, the teacher was ready for her fantastic voyage. Her task was to conduct two fifteen-minute classes in space as millions of schoolchildren watched via closed circuit television. She would explain the functioning of the shuttle and the benefits of space travel.

She never got the chance to do what she loved best, which was to teach. Nowhere was the tragedy felt more than in Concord, where fellow teachers and pupils had gathered inside the school auditorium to watch what they had presumed to be their colleague and friend's moment of triumph.

Throughout the town, the thirty thousand residents were engulfed by sorrow as the news quickly spread. 'People froze in their tracks,' said one local. 'It was like part of the family has been killed.'

American music was played on Soviet state-run radio, and officials in Moscw announced they were naming craters on

Venus in honour of the two female crew members, McAuliffe and Resnik.

In Vatican City, Pope John Paul II asked an audience of thousands to pray for the American astronauts, saying that the tragedy had 'provoked deep sorrow in my soul'. British Premier Margaret Thatcher sadly observed that 'New knowledge sometimes demands sacrifices of the bravest and the best.'

And Senator John Glenn, the first American to orbit the earth, recalled: 'The first group of us always knew there would be a day like this. We're dealing with speeds and powers and complexities we've never dealt with before.'

Across the United States, communities reacted in their own ways to the news. In Los Angeles, the Olympic torch atop the Coliseum was relit. New York City's Empire State Building was darkened. And along the Florida coast an estimated twenty-two thousand people pointed torches at the sky.

THE INVESTIGATION

As the nation grieved, back at Cape Canaveral the US Coast Guard and NASA crews had already began the grim task of searching for the wreckage of *Challenger*.

They had to wait almost sixty minutes after the explosion before starting the search, because of debris still raining from the sky. Their search covered some six thousand square miles of the Atlantic.

Despite the power of the blast, searchers began finding surprisingly large parts of the wreckage scattered on the ocean floor, including a 25 ft long section of the *Challenger*'s fuselage.

As for the astronauts themselves, it was only after extensive prodding that NASA admitted that the crew had not perished instantly, as initially claimed. They survived the explosion and probably lived until their cabin hit the surface of the ocean.

Once the wreckage had been gathered, NASA investigators began the arduous task of finding out what had gone wrong. It was a three-pronged probe. First, there was the film to study from eighty NASA cameras and ninety belonging to news organizations. There were also the billions of computer signals sent between the doomed craft and its earthbound control centres. And lastly, there were the actual remains of the *Challenger*.

There was speculation that ice, which had formed on the launch pad the night before the lift-off, had damaged the craft - as the engineer at Rockwell had feared.

Also suspected was that the external fuel tank's insulation had been damaged during a minor accident a few days earlier, when a derrick arm supposedly scraped the tank. But NASA insisted the derrick had touched not the tank, but only part of the launch-pad equipment.

Speculation soon centred on the possibility of a failure in either the main tank or one of the two booster rockets. Experts noted that either could have caused the violent explosion. Another possibility was that a seam in the main tank had ruptured.

In closed meetings, a specially constituted panel began to grill top NASA officials as well as engineers from Morton Thiokol, the company that makes the solid fuel boosters suspected of triggering the disaster. What they uncovered stunned the commissioners.

The engineers had adamantly opposed the launch because of the icy weather at Cape Canaveral.

Robert Sieck, the shuttle manager at the Kennedy Space Center, and Gene Thomas, the launch director for *Challenger* at Kennedy, testified that they had never before heard that Thiokol engineers had objected to the launch.

Gradually, most rocket experts agreed that at least one of the two synthetic rubber O-rings that were meant to seal the joint between the booster's four segments had begun to burn. About 1/4 in thick, and some 37 feet in circumference, the O-rings are designed to keep the rocket's exhaust gases from escaping through any gaps in the joints.

The evening before the launch, Thiokol engineers and NASA officials met to discuss the potential problems. The engineers were unanimous in asking for the *Challenger* launch to be delayed.

They were worried that the O-rings might lose some of their elasticity, and hence their ability to sit tightly in their grooves around the rockets, when their temperature fell below 50 degrees. That evening the temperature was 30 degrees.

Eventually, however, Morton Thiokol senior vice-president Jerald Mason declared that 'We have to make a management decision.' He and three other Thiokol vice-presidents, approved the launch.

But Allan McDonald, director of Thiokol's engineers after 'heated exchanges' with NASA officials, refused to sign an official approval to proceed. 'I argued before, and I argued after,' he told reporters.

Below: *Plumes of smoke follow segments of the space shuttle which hurtled rocket debris to earth in several directions.*

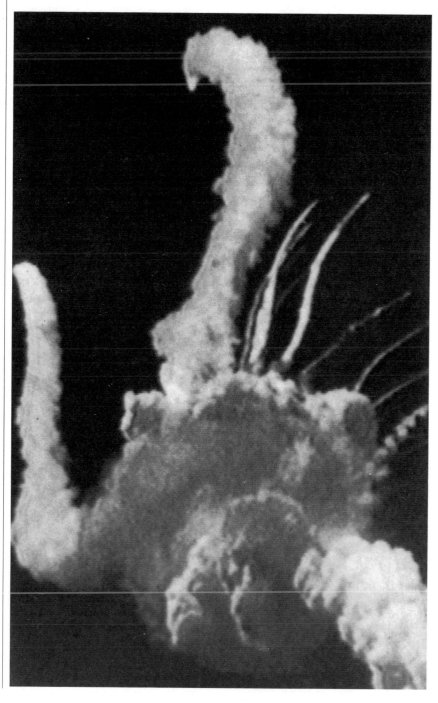

NASA, it seemed, was not interested in 'fears', but instead demanded proof that the launch would be unsafe. At one point, a NASA official supposedly asked the engineers: 'My God, when do you want me to launch, next April?' Finally NASA over-ruled the engineers.

NASA, it seems, was not interested in fears of an unsafe launch - only in proof. Tragically, they got it

---

Incredibly, on the morning of the actual launch NASA missed another chance to abort the launch. Icicles had formed on the huge tower that supports the craft on the launch pad and Space Agency officials - concerned that ice breaking off might damage the heat shield tiles - sent in the 'ice teams' to inspect the pad three times.

Information in one of the reports about abnormal 'cold spots' on the right booster rocket was somehow missed. That meant that its O-rings were subjected to far greater cold than on any previous flight.

THE FINDINGS

At a public hearing of the Senate Subcommittee on Science, Technology and Space, Senator Ernest Hollings said of the disaster: 'At this particular juncture it seems like an avoidable accident rather than an unavoidable one.'

Later, he would charge that it was becoming 'apparent that NASA made a political decision to go ahead with [the] launch...despite strong objections.'

It was later revealed that since at least 1980 NASA had recognized that the seals between the booster sections were cause for concern.

On the first twelve shuttle flights, in four instances the O-rings had been partly burned away. Afterwards, the Space Agency began using a new type of putty to protect the joint - with the result that erosion of O-rings then occurred even more frequently.

Despite all the evidence NASA's top engineers and managers judged that this flaw was not serious enough to halt or delay shuttle flights.

The safety panel concluded that the tragedy had been caused by the 'failure of the pressure seal in the aft-field joint of the right solid-rocket motor', but noted that 'there was a serious flaw in the decision-making process'.

The panel was reluctant to assign personal blame for the tragedy, but instead outlined recommendations to ensure that such a disaster never happened again.

Its 285-page report to President Reagan urged that the shuttle's booster joints be entirely redesigned rather than just modified and that all the shuttle's critical parts be reviewed.

In addition, NASA had been eager to get the Challenger into orbit because of a series of earlier postponements to the original launch date three days before, on Saturday 25 January. First there was a dust storm at the emergency landing site in Senegal. Then, at Cape Canaveral, it rained, which could damage the heat-resistant tiles on the spacecraft. And on Monday, first a stuck bolt on an exterior-hatch handle, then 35mph winds delayed the launch until the next morning.

But the commission did not lay the blame entirely at NASA's feet. It also noted that the numbers of flights it had proposed had never been adequately funded by Washington, and that its budget had been so heavily slashed that even spare parts were running low.

AFTERMATH

Four days later, on the Friday, America held its final farewell for the Seven. Under grey skies at the Johnson Space Center near Houston, where they had trained, some six thousand NASA employees, congressmen and relatives gathered to hear President Reagan.

The sacrifice of your loved ones has stirred the soul of our nation, and, through the pain, our hearts have been opened to a profound truth: the future is not free...

Dick, Mike, Judy, El, Ron, Greg and Christa, your families and your country mourn your passing. We bid you goodbye, but we will never forget you.

The American people certainly would not let NASA forget them. The Space

Agency, once a source of national pride, was subjected to lengthy overhauls and reviews determined to ensure, as far as modern technology and human errors would allow, that there would never again be a disaster like the *Challenger*.

The entire shuttle programme was also revamped and many changes made to the existing fleet. On 29 September 1988 there was a collective sigh of relief at the dramatically successful flight of the space shuttle *Discovery*, which marked America's return to manned space flight after a thirty-two-month break.

Not surprisingly, given their woes in the wake of the *Challenger* disaster, NASA officials treated the *Discovery* mission as if it were the test flight of a brand-new vehicle. Engineers estimated that four times as much work went into the new design as had gone into the original development in the mid-1970s.

The main engines located at the tail of the shuttle had been plagued by problems from the beginning, and during the enforced hiatus NASA made thirty-five changes to them.

The razzmatazz of the space shuttle should be put aside, urged the panel, in favour of more sensible scientific projects

---

NASA's engineers made 210 changes to the design of the orbiter itself and another 100 modifications to its highly sophisticated computer software.

But in the ensuing three years the shuttle programme was plagued by major and minor problems, putting increased pressure on the workload. In 1991 a panel concluded in a report to the White House that NASA should focus on new goals in the wake of budget cuts, the recession and its own ineptitude.

The report strongly suggested that the Agency should not spend funds buying another after the *Endeavor* joined the current fleet of three later that year. It concluded that another tragic and disastrous shuttle accident was highly probable by the end of the century.

Other points raised were putting research and development ahead of splashy TV space extravaganzas, and not

risking astronauts when robots can do the same job. NASA was told to cut costs and get back to more scientific missions.

The shuttle has been plagued by glitches in the early 1990s - everything from computer failures to clogged toilets. And the entire fleet was once grounded for five months by a dangerous fuel leak.

Still, experts say that the shuttle will play an integral part in the construction of the space station Freedom – the first step in America's plan to put a man on Mars before the year 2015.

Below: *Horror is frozen on the faces of watchers in the VIP area at Kennedy Space Center as the craft explodes 72 seconds after ignition.*

EXXON VALDEZ
Oil Spill Catastrophe

On 24 March 1989 the clear waters of Prince William Sound in Alaska became hideously polluted as the supertanker Exxon Valdez hit a reef. Ten million gallons of stinking black crude escaped after the accident that arrogant oil barons had said could never happen

laskan Eskimos are steeped in the traditions and beliefs of their forefathers. One of their deities is Sedna, goddess of the sea, a powerful ruler who deserved much homage to keep the ocean's harvest of seals and fish - the Eskimo lifeblood - well nurtured. The goddess is fabled for her distaste for man and his 'filth'.

THE CAPTAIN WITH A DRINK PROBLEM

Environmental agencies and government legislation had gone to great lengths - far more than in other American states - to keep the straits, lakes and seaways fresh and beautiful. But in 1989 Sedna suffered the most heinous blow ever delivered by a mortal against a god when a ship called the *Exxon Valdez* ran aground in one of the most unpolluted stretches of water in the world.

The goddess's distaste was justified - man had committed one of the world's worst acts of pollution, spewing millions of gallons of crude oil into the sparkling, clear waters.

The 'big spill', as the locals now call it, occurred at precisely four minutes past midnight on 24 March 1989 when Captain Joseph Hazelwood, master of the supertanker *Exxon Valdez*, was absent from the bridge.

At forty-two, Captain Hazelwood, was

Above: *The tanker* **Exxon San Francisco** *is pushed by tugs up against the stricken* **Valdez** *as work begins to salvage the oil remaining aboard her.*

Opposite: *Snow-peaked mountains dwarf the* **Exxon Valdez.**

Left: *The* **Exxon Valdez** *spewed 10 million gallons of oil into the sea when it ran aground on a reef in Prince William Sound.*

at the peak of his career with Exxon and earned around £100,000 a year as one of its star captains. He had wealth, responsibility, respect...and a drinking problem which would lead the ship to tragedy on that chill, starlit night.

The discovery of oil in the remote state of Alaska in 1968 had been a boon to the locals, whose only other sources of income were fishing, hunting and tourism. The oil revenues had reduced state taxes, and there were good wages to be earned as the black gold continued to flow into the bellies of the supertankers.

But with oil came a change in the bucolic way of life that the locals had enjoyed cheek-by-jowl with the native Eskimos for centuries. As well as the ever-present risk of an accident, the tough world of oilmen and sailors had stripped the area of its innocent charm for ever.

The current boom in communities like Valdez, on Prince William Sound, was the result of years of bickering and bitter argument about how best to move the oil three thousand miles and more to the thirsty markets awaiting it. The companies drilling for it had examined many different options, including building a pipeline through Canada to California and the Mid-West.

Captains of the US oil industry, though, were not best pleased with the prospect of moving American resources across foreign territory. In the end the trans-Alaska companies and the federal government settled on a pipeline that brought the oil down to Valdez from the permafrost fields further north.

The Valdez pipeline is a magnificent feat of engineering running for nearly eight hundred miles across the Arctic wilderness

---

That 789-mile pipeline is one of the most remarkable engineering feats in history - 101,850 sections of 48-in diameter steel pipe going through rivers and lakes and across Arctic ranges.

Once loaded on board ships like the *Exxon Valdez* it was transported to Texan or Californian ports for refining.

In the early evening of 23 March the *Exxon Valdez* was loading up with 1.26 million barrels of oil.

Captain Hazelwood, the third mate Gregory Cousins and Robert Kagan, the helmsman, were the only crewmen to leave the ship. Against all rules that forbade drinking at sea - and an Exxon regulation which prohibited the consumption of alcohol for at least four hours before a journey was started - Hazelwood and the two others went to sink some beers at the Pipeline Club. Later, eye-witnesses would report that they had seen him drink at least four beers. Hazelwood's employers knew about his previous drinking bouts and had once sent him to a drying-out clinic.

James Shiminski, an Exxon chief mate, said: 'He had a reputation for both partying ashore and on board the ship.'

In 1984 Hazelwood was convicted for drunken driving after a car crash.

A year later he underwent a twenty-eight-day stay in an alcohol addiction clinic not far from his home on Long Island, New York.

THE FATEFUL JOURNEY BEGINS

Within an hour of his latest drinking session Hazelwood and his party had returned to the dockside ready to board the vessel for sailing.

At 9.10pm he was on the bridge of the *Exxon Valdez* as she slipped her moorings for Long Beach, California, where a substantial refinery complex would process her cargo.

William Murphy was the harbour pilot who was obliged by law to navigate the ship for the two hours it took to weave through the shallow sea lane littered with jagged rocks. Later he would tell investigators that he smelled alcohol on the skipper's breath that night but that his demeanour did not indicate that he was intoxicated.

The ship, bigger than three football pitches end to end, lumbered off into the still, freezing night an hour before her scheduled sailing time. In the bowels of the ship engines capable of producing over 35,000 horsepower pushed her on her way.

Shortly after 11.30pm, only minutes after the pilot Murphy had left the bridge and returned home on a harbour launch, Hazelwood radioed the local coastguard and said he was altering the course of the ship from the outward, ice-infested channel to the inbound, ice-free channel.

At approximately 11.50pm Hazelwood turned over the bridge, and therefore control of the ship, to the third mate, Cousins. The second mate, Lloyd

Below: *The* **Valdez** *caused an environmental disaster ecologists had been warning about for 15 years - and which oil companies said was 'impossible'.*

LeCaine, was in a deep sleep.

Regulations stated that it was LeCaine who should have assumed the responsibility. However, maritime experts have since concurred it was a rule more often broken than observed by many skippers.

The coastguard had to give permission for the turn into the inbound channel - which it did - but shortly afterwards lost radar contact with the ship. Hazelwood had told Cousins to make a right turn back into the outbound channel when the vessel reached a navigational point near Busby Island, three miles north of a jagged underwater outcrop of rock called Bligh Reef.

The captain was just fifteen feet away from the bridge, completing paperwork in his cabin, when disaster struck. The *Exxon Valdez* was more than a mile from where she should have been.

One reason could have been that helmsman Robert Kagan, feeling that the ship was turning too sharply back towards the outbound channel, used a counter-rudder manoeuvre to slow the swing. Such a measure was logged in the ship's course recorder, a kind of maritime 'black box'.

Captain Hazlewood heard the groaning of tortured steel beneath him.

Cousins repeated the order for a hard-right rudder, and then Captain Hazelwood felt the groaning and twisting of steel underneath him and knew that something had gone terribly, terribly wrong. Then came the phone call from Cousins: 'We are in trouble!'

Hazelwood bolted to the bridge and knew instantly from the lack of motion that the ship had grounded on the reef and was hanging precariously like a gigantic see-saw. His first job was to make sure it didn't slip off the reef, which could cause her either to keel over or to break her back. Hazelwood was in for the longest night of his life.

Beneath his 987-ft-long ship were huge rents in her steel hull, some fifteen feet long. Eight of the fifteen cargo holds were ruptured, and in time some 240,000 barrels of oil, forty-two gallons in each,

would be released into the sound with catastrophic effect.

Despite some question marks over Hazelwood's sobriety or otherwise, investigators would later say he showed excellent seamanship in his efforts at damage limitation. By adjusting the engine power he was able to keep the vessel firmly pressed up against the reef and stable.

Once the *Exxon Valdez* had run aground she was picked up again by the coastguard radar. In what seems to have been a case of bureaucratic bungling, the coastguards did not board the stricken ship until three hours later.

THE BUNGLED CLEAN-UP

Daylight brought with it full realization of the environmental horror that had occurred. Already the carcasses of sea otters and birds had begun to be seen on the outer reaches of the spill.

First the coastguards lost touch with the ship on their radar, then it took them three hours to reach her after she grounded

---

The scene was the environmental disaster that protesters had been warning of for years. But two years before the disaster the consortium of powerful oil companies had said haughtily: 'It is highly unlikely that there will ever be a spill of any magnitude.'

The consortium further boasted that slick-fighting materials would be on hand within five hours to neutralize the effects of any spill.

But the first clean-up crews did not get to the spill site until ten hours afterwards, during which time the 10 million-plus gallons gurgling from the shattered hull of the *Exxon Valdez* continued unabated into the sound. And even then they were pitifully inadequately equipped to deal with a spillage of such major proportions.

They had been lulled into complacency even though their equipment had been proved taxed to the limit in dealing with a small spill of just 1500 barrels in January the same year. There were no

Below: One of the several oil cargo tanks aboard the 987-foot **Valdez***. Workers removed 1600 tons of damaged steel from the ship's hull before putting her back in service.*

booms to contain the spreading slick and few skimmers, which swept the surface of the water collecting oil.

All the equipment to deal with the vast slick was inadequate or out of action

---

The slick was still spreading, but chemicals could not be used because the water was calm, which rendered them ineffective. The coastguard, which by law was supposed to have vessels on hand capable of dealing with a 'major' spill, had its minuscule fleet of ships two thousand miles away in San Francisco.

By Sunday, 26 March, winds had picked up across the sound and were whipping the surface oil into a 'mousse' - a frothy cream that defied attempts to skim it up. Attempts were made to burn it, also to no avail.

The oil had now formed the biggest slick in history – covering 900 square miles, fouling the inlets that are home to sea otters, the nesting shallows of dozens of bird species and the once-pristine beaches where seals suckled their young.

At the last count the body count was grim: 86,000 birds, among them 139 rare bald eagles, 984 sea otters, 25,000 fish, 200 seals and several dozen beavers were the victims. Millions of mussels, sea urchins and other forms of marine life were wiped out for ever. Thousands more sea otters are feared to be dead, their bodies weighted down with oil to sink for ever beneath the surface.

Some beaches had to be treated with detergent chemicals seven times

---

Some beaches had to be treated seven times with detergents and other chemicals. Environmental scientist Paul Willard said:

The spill happened in almost the worst place possible. The jagged coast of Prince William Sound is dotted with innumerable coves and inlets where the spilled oil collected and stayed for months, killing young fish that spawn in the shallows.

LAWSUITS

Exxon came under a barrage of criticism. Newspaper advertisements urged people not to buy Exxon products and their service stations were deserted, the result of national disgust at their seemingly cavalier treatment of the disaster.

Exxon's President, Frank Iarossi, countered with the pledge of a billion dollars for the clean-up. Exxon also made a commitment to compensate fishermen and others who had directly suffered because of the spill.

In apportioning blame for the big spill it has been all too easy merely to point the finger at Captain Hazelwood and his love for a drink too many. He was fired almost immediately after the disaster. Exxon cited as their reason positive blood alcohol tests taken nine hours after the ship grounded. But subsequent inquiries have concluded that he acted honourably afterwards and with great skill, and that he may only have gone over the limit afterwards when he needed to steady his nerves.

The fatigue of his crew, as much as the combination of errors in navigation that night, may well have played a part in the grounding of the *Exxon Valdez*. There were just twenty crewmen working that night on board one of the biggest vessels afloat - a reduction of twenty-four from when Hazelwood had first sailed in her.

Also at fault were the coastguards who, had they not lost the ship on their radar, might well have been able to notify her that she was navigating into dangerous waters.

New, more stringent alcohol rules have been applied in the disaster's wake, and double-hulled vessels are replacing single-hulled ones operating in the sound. But for those who live there, and for the defiled goddess Sedna, it is all a matter of too little, too late.

Above: *Oil from the stricken tanker is pumped aboard its sister ship the* **Exxon Baton Rouge** *as clean-up efforts continued on the oil spill in Prince William Sound.*

SAN FRANCISCO
Rocked by Earthquakes

Perched astride the San Andreas Fault, San Francisco has suffered two horrific earthquakes this century. But the Big One, the one that will utterly destroy this beautiful city, is still to come - and that fate is inevitable

Opposite: *The smouldering rubble of an apartment building in San Francisco's Marina district after the 1989 earthquake struck.*

Below: *The devastated main shopping centre, with famous Telegraph Hill in the background, in 1906.*

Bottom: *Crowds watch part of old San Francisco go up in smoke.*

Tony Bennett left his heart in it, Al Jolson begged it to 'open up that Golden Gate', and a generation of hippies were urged to put flowers in their hair when they visited it.

San Francisco's splendid vistas and its old European-style houses and plazas, serviced by a quaint cable-car network from another age, combine to make the city by the bay one of the most splendid and 'livable' of all the great American metropolises. In art, culture and social tolerance - it is home to America's biggest gay community as well as the nation's most rapidly expanding Asian

and Japanese districts - San Francisco stands out.

Only one force - a massive, irresistible force - stands in the way of the Utopia which San Francisco has become for so many people. And that force is nature.

A CATASTROPHE BOUND TO HAPPEN

Twice this century - in 1906 and in 1989 - nature has flexed its considerable muscles to prove itself more powerful than the most reinforced of reinforced concrete, not to mention the strongest of tungsten steel.

But the two earthquakes which wrought havoc on San Francisco are only the precursors of the the ultimate Big

One - the one which will level this beautiful man-made monument. This is not a Nostradamus-type prediction; the city's location dictates that one day it will crumble, burn and disappear into great fissures, to linger only as a memory.

Imagine two badly stacked dinner plates with a delicate wineglass on top - the wineglass is San Francisco

---

The reason for the city's ultimate demise lies in a mammoth geological hiccup spawned in the days when the earth itself was formed. Called the San Andreas Fault, it is literally a 650-mile-long crack in the earth where the Pacific plate is slowly but surely sliding underneath the landmass of California, itself part of the North America plate.

Scientists say one way for the human mind to grasp what is happening is to put two dinner plates on top of one another and move them so they overlap at each side. Place a full wine glass on the top plate and move the bottom one. Slow movements will cause the wine to shake - more energetic ones to make it spill over the top. The most violent wrench of all will see the glass and contents topple, spill and smash. That is the fate that awaits San Francisco.

This is not to scaremonger - the Big One could come next year or in a thousand years' time. All that is certain is that it will eventually come.

REHEARSAL

The first massive quake to devastate San Francisco occurred on 18 April 1906. When the first shock waves were felt the natives of the gold rush town that grew into the West Coast's most thriving community were blasé about it. Tremors happened a lot there - still do, in fact - and it was not uncommon to feel a rumbling beneath your feet or to watch the table cruet dance before your eyes.

Indeed, on that fateful day, when the newspaper magnate William Randolph Hearst was awakened in his ornate New York apartment to be told that his beloved native San Francisco was being consumed by earthquake and fire, he

Above: *A 1906 photograph of the corner of South Market Street and Main Street.*

Right: *Helpers set up an open-air canteen amid the devastation of San Francisco.*

replied: 'Don't overplay it - they often have earthquakes over in California.'

The San Francisco earthquake was sadly everything, and more, that his minion had told him - the single most cataclysmic event of the age.

'Don't overplay it,' said William Randolph Hearst, when first informed of the 1906 quake

---

The quake is estimated to have registered 8.3 on the Richter scale, the yardstick for seismic measurements, although it was only an estimate as the measurement system had not been devised then. That force is greater than thirty nuclear underground blasts triggered simultaneously. Eight hundred people perished in the collapsing buildings and the chasms which opened up in the streets, or in the firestorm which swiftly consumed the wooden buildings in the aftermath of the vibrations.

Mary Monti, now ninety-four, recalled the events of that grim day.

It knocked me out of bed. The walls of the house we lived in shook and then cracked - great spider's web cracks as the plaster crumbled with the force. We ran into the street and the surface of the road was boiling and rolling. My mother grabbed us kids and we got out of town on a cart, into the hills. Everywhere there was fire. Suddenly a new fire would start up as gas mains got ruptured or kerosene was spilled.

She was one of three hundred thousand people made homeless by the devastating natural disaster which destroyed close to twenty-nine thousand buildings.

On Telegraph Hill Italian families tried to douse the flames with ten thousand gallons of wine

---

The quake had destroyed water lines as well as gas pipes, so firemen could not tackle the blazes. On Telegraph Hill, one of the more celebrated promontories in the city, Italian immigrant families wasted ten thousand gallons of wine which they poured on to the flames.

Packs of looters roamed the streets, robbing shattered stores and stealing from the dead who lined the gutters. And from the few remaining lampstands hung those robbers who were caught by tearful and vengeful citizens.

The author, Jack London, wrote a moving account of the disaster for Collier's weekly magazine:*San Francisco is gone!...On Wednesday morning at a quarter past five came the earthquake. A minute later the flames were leaping upward. In a dozen different quarters south of Market Street, in the working class ghetto, and in the factories, fire started. There was no opposing the flames. There was no organization, no communication...all the shrewd contrivances and safeguards of man had been thrown out of gear by thirty seconds twitching of the earth's crust.*

By the time the fires burned out more than 75 per cent of San Francisco was destroyed, four hundred city blocks in ruins. It provoked scientists and government to pour money into researching the massive fault and what could be done to predict the next quake.

EARTHQUAKE TECHNOLOGY

At the time of the earthquake, geologists had only a sketchy understanding of the processes that combine to move and shake the earth. They realized that the disaster was linked to the San Andreas Fault, and that the land to the west of the faultline was edging northwards.

A geologist from Pennsylvania, Harry Fielding Reid, observing twisted fence posts and shattered roadways, found that there had been a ground lurch of as much as 21 feet during the quake.

More importantly, he recognized that the great blocks of earth on either side of the faultline had been under tremendous strain long before the earthquake happened. Tremendous friction had caused two faces of the fault to stick until

Below: *A rare, early photograph of one of the pioneers who founded San Francisco in 1849.*

Above: *A dramatic photograph of San Francisco's ruined skyline after the earthquake and ensuing fire storm swept the city in 1906.*

the accumulating forces were at last released with a massive snap.

In the 1970s scientists recognized that different sections along the San Andreas Fault were moving at different rates, causing strain to build up in some areas more than others. From Point Arena to San Juan Bautista, a small town south of San Francisco, and from Parkfield down to the Mexican border, the fault is stuck.

When the tremendous force has built up and the fault moves - then the next earthquake is born. California quake expert William Bakun says:

First and foremost we want to learn the earthquake generation process. Then we want to learn how to predict them in areas where they are a hazard.

Sadly, it is still not an exact science, although the colleges and universities of California lead the world in earthquake technology. Another quake expert, David Langston, said:

All we can do is to keep on trying to predict and hope we improve sufficiently to give the population a fair warning when a huge quake is on its way and not be accused of crying wolf.

Following hard on those studies, in 1980 the Federal Emergency Management Agency worked out a scenario that earthquakes would strike at both San Francisco and Los Angeles. Their findings were grim, with death predictions topping fifty thousand in the San Francisco quake and property

damage at over $20 million. The worst case scenario says that in the quake's wake will be a wasteland of fires and looting, with possible disease rife in the breakdown of law and order.

In 1989 a TV-age disaster dramatically set the scene for what will one day befall the city on a much larger scale.

FURTHER WARNING

In the words of housewife Annette Henry, who was in one of the city's main thoroughfares when it struck, here is what the great quake of October 1989 felt like: 'It was as if God just clapped his hands. The ground was like a wave underneath a surfboard, and the cars on the highway were jumping up and down like in a Disney movie. Every time we have an earthquake in California we giggle, we're cool, we're blasé about it. This time was different. I was just hanging on thinking, it's not so funny any more. I thought we were having the Big One.'

'The cars on the highway were jumping up and down like a Disney movie'

Rocks in the San Andreas Fault couldn't stand the pressure any longer and 58,000-foot-thick blocks of the earth's crust heaved violently. Pressure waves, travelling at five miles per second, raced from the quake's epicentre,

south-east of San Francisco through the bedrock under the Santa Cruz Mountains.

It hit San Francisco during the evening rush hour of Tuesday, 17 October and within fifteen seconds had reduced many buildings to rubble, had destroyed a section of the Bay Bridge, collapsed over a mile of elevated highway, and left the historic Marina district engulfed by fire.

Thanks to global TV coverage of the World Series baseball game between the Oakland A's and San Francisco Giants, viewers as far away as London witnessed the first shocks as the Candlestick Park stadium visibly swayed and huge cracks appeared in the concrete walls.

Most of the hundred deaths from the earthquake occurred when a mile-long section of Interstate 880, an elevated freeway, collapsed on to the lower roadway. Dozens of people were trapped in their cars that were concertinaed together by tons of reinforced concrete.

'It just sandwiched in,' said Henry Reniera, manager for emergency services for Oakland.

It is like a war zone out there. The upper deck fell like a hammer blow on to the lower deck, showering motorists below with rubble and cars. Trapped victims beneath tons of debris have been frantically honking their horns and we are rushing in massive amounts of lifting equipment and hydraulic jacks in a bid to get to them. It is an eerie sound, muffled horns that slowly fade as the car batteries run flat and you know that humans are trapped in there.

The most moving rescue of the entire disaster occurred in the rubble beneath the collapsed Nimitz Freeway section. Patrick Wallace, a paper mill worker, was one of the first on the scene to the sandwiched cars and heard the terrified screams of children trapped in a red car. Together with other rescuers he was able to help free an eight-year-old girl, Cathy Berumen, but her six-year-old brother Julio was trapped - pinned in the wreckage by the body of his dead mother.

Risking his life from further after-shocks, Dr Dan Allen crawled through a three-foot gap to give sedatives to Julio until another doctor, a childcare specialist, could climb up a fire truck's ladders.

Dr Thomas Betts said: 'Nothing could have prepared me for what I saw there. The boy was in shock. He would just cry and run his hands over his mother's face.'

After two hours of frantic work the medical team were no nearer to getting Julio free. His right leg was crushed beyond repair and they needed to get him out for immediate treatment. The boy was put under sedation while a chainsaw was deployed to cut his mother in half before his own leg was amputated.

As fires blazed through the night, glass popped from the twisted skyscrapers built without earthquake specifications and the sirens wailed eerily across the city, the politicians and planners did have some

cause for comfort. Initial reports proved that the destruction was intensely localized, concentrated in older structures that had not been upgraded to withstand earthquakes. The collapsed highway section, which claimed most lives, was itself thirty years old.

Experts concurred that the strict Californian building code - instituted after the 1906 disaster in a bid to minimize damage in future quakes and updated in the late eighties to incorporate the lessons learned from the 1971 San Fernando and 1985 Mexico City quakes - played a large part in minimizing the damage.

But there is no denying the inevitability of the scale of disaster if a new quake hits the 8.3 Richter scale reading of the 1906 one. A study made by the National Oceanic and Atmospheric Administration after the quake concluded that forty times as much energy would be released as in the 1989 one, resulting in thousands upon thousands of deaths.

San Franciscans are still clearing up the mess of the quake, a process which will

Above: *San Francisco's elegant, wooden houses burn after the 1989 quake.*

Below: *This scene of devastation was once a six-lane highway. It was reduced to twisted metal and shattered concrete.*

take the best part of ten years to complete. They are proud of having come through, and flaunt their fatalistic attitude to nature's aggression. The columnist for the *San Francisco Chronicle*, Herb Caen, summed up the city by the bay when he wrote in the days after the quake: 'We live with earthquakes and we live on a fault and we live dangerously. And it's exciting.'